Weapons of Peace

The Story of William & Johanna Anderson

by Peter S. Anderson

Weapons of Peace
— The Story of William & Johanna Anderson

© 1995, 2016 by Peter S. Anderson
peter.anderson@slingshot.co.nz
First Edition (1995) Design and Production by
Logos Production House, Hong Kong
Second Edition (2016) Design and Production by
Our Daily Bread Ministries

Editor: Leslie Koh – Our Daily Bread Ministries
Cover & Interior Design: Mary Chang – Our Daily Bread Ministries

Requests for permission to quote from this book
should be directed to the author

Scripture is from the New International Version,
© 1978 by New York International Bible Society,
Hodder and Stoughton.

ISBN 962-457-091-4

Printed in Indonesia
Second printing in 2016

Table of Content

Foreword

*W*eapons of Peace" is a godly, and beautifully written story of high missionary adventure, courage, sacrifice, and faithful perseverance. In this splendidly researched and sensitively scripted saga of his two great missionary ancestors, William and Johanna Anderson, the author brings into purview for his readers a vivid, moving, sometimes heart-rending but always inspiring picture of pioneer missionary work in South Africa in the first half of the nineteenth century.

Here we meet first-hand the faith, raw courage, pain, hardship and spirit of perseverance which laid the foundations we so often take for granted in the thriving modern church we see in South Africa today. But there would be no such church but for the astonishing labours of people like William and Johanna Anderson – proclaimers, prophets, pastors, and peacemakers extraordinary – who paid the price of fifty years of Gospel faithfulness, amidst unbelievable hardship, to bring the message of Christ to African peoples who had never heard. Ministering in an age of very limited medical help or knowledge, of totally primitive transport when it took two months to go by ox wagon, a journey now taking a day by car, and in absence of any of the comforts and protections of modern life, these intrepid missionary pioneers rebuke us moderns in our shallow and comfortable commitment, our easy compromises on biblical authority, and our love of ease.

Beyond that, these early pioneers like William and Johanna show us what holistic ministry is all about with their fervent evangelising, their dedicated discipling of converts, their unflagging educational and civilising labours, their practical care, and their prophetic stance for justice and reconciliation.

These were their "weapons of peace" indeed and they wielded them with consummate skill. How they did it is still instructive for us today who build on their labours.

I believe Peter Anderson has also given us here a particularly useful and almost timeless study tool for any going into cross-cultural ministries in our time. So I hope this volume will have a readership in Bible Schools or even Seminaries where students are preparing for such work.

And for flagging or discouraged Christian workers in church or para-church organisations who are longing, as William was in 1840, "to finish my course with joy and remain faithful to the end", there are clues abundant in these pages as to how he and Johanna did it. One especially registers their unswerving commitment to Jesus Christ, their faithful and tenacious praying, their resolute determination to endure unto the end, and their utter devotion to the Bible. "It gives me all the comfort and strength I need," said William near the end of his life.

So I commend to one and all this tender but telling and triumphant tale of adventure and high achievement for our Lord Jesus Christ. Read and be inspired. I was.

—**Michael Cassidy**, *Founder and International Team Leader, African Enterprise, Pietermaritzburg, April 1995*

Other Commendations for Weapons of Peace

Peter Anderson's imaginative and gripping biography about our courageous ancestors is the result of his careful archival research and personal knowledge. Set in the early 19th Century and grounded in historical fact, it depicts the beginnings of the long evangelical missionary heritage of the Anderson family in Southern Africa.
—*Professor **Allan Anderson**, University of Birmingham, England*

I found "Weapons of Peace" very encouraging and profound. I know the Anderson Family intimately, as my son is married to a beautiful Anderson girl. They are a God-fearing people who love Jesus passionately! I heartily recommend this book as a faith builder to encourage God's people to pursue their God-given vision and dream, knowing that He will never leave nor forsake them. (Hebrew 13:5).
—***Angus Buchan, South African farmer,** evangelist and author ("Faith Like Potatoes"), and founder of Shalom Ministries.*

Peter Anderson rises admirably to the challenge of using the detailed letters and reports of his long-serving missionary ancestors, alongside other historical research. He has produced an engagingly readable exploration of William and Johanna Anderson's work among both Griqua and Khoi, employing 'weapons of peace' in often fraught and complicated early nineteenth-century Christian encounters.
—***Dr. Deborah Gaitskell,** Research Associate, School of Oriental and African Studies, London*

This thrilling book moved, enlightened and delighted me! William Anderson was one of the great early pioneers of the modern missionary movement, but few know about his pioneer ministry among the Griqua people and beyond and his vital contribution to the establishment of the Gospel in Southern Africa. Peter Anderson, a sixth generation descendent, has carefully researched and colourfully portrayed the personalities involved to produce this gem of a biography.
—**Patrick Johnstone,** *WEC International, Author Emeritus, Operation World*

The seasons of life and ministry lie exposed within these pages: conflict, revival, failure, fruitfulness, suffering, and sin. And then we discover two people inhabiting those seasons with a stubborn commitment to dignity, reconciliation, and peace. This creates a story of realism and tenderness with a resonance in our times and cultures.
—**Dr. Paul Windsor,** *Director of Langham Preaching and former Principal of Carey Baptist College, Auckland, New Zealand.*

Preface

*W*eapons of Peace" is a human drama set in early nineteenth century South Africa. It tells the story of William and Johanna Anderson. William was one of the very earliest missionaries of the London Missionary Society (L.M.S.) and served in Africa for over fifty years. John Bond, in his 1956 book "They Were South Africans", dedicates a whole chapter to him. William was indeed one of the great pioneers of South Africa, a true friend and champion of the coloured and indigenous peoples of the sub-continent. Reporting his passing, a lengthy tribute appeared in the major newspaper of the Cape, the South African Commercial Advertiser, on 2 October 1852. It spoke of William as a man "of indomitable courage, and boundless benevolence. His name is revered by the races whom he first led into the paths of civilized life, by pouring upon their minds the light of the eternal world." Johanna, of Dutch and Huguenot descent, stood with her husband through all the joys and trials of their life together – a woman of deep faith and courage. Their story is one with powerful relevance even at the end of the twentieth century.

Though written as a novel, "Weapons of Peace" is strictly true to historical fact. A wealth of material was gleaned from the letters and journals of William Anderson and others in the excellent archives of the Council for World Mission (formerly London Missionary Society) housed in the library of London University's School of Oriental and African Studies. Much helpful information was also obtained from "The Harvest and the Hope – the story of Congregationalism in Southern Africa" by Roy Briggs and Joseph Wing, as well as from various other histories. It was my own grandfather, Rev. William Wardlaw Anderson, himself a great-grandson of William and Johanna, who sparked my own interest in this great story.

Special thanks to those who spent time checking the manuscript – Barry and Joy Payne, Reg Dismore, Mary Stevens, Dr Ruth Plummer, and Maureen Brownlow, as well as my parents Alec and Kath Anderson. I am particularly grateful to Michael Cassidy of African Enterprise for so kindly doing the foreword and to Graham and Santie McIntosh for their support. Last, but not least, my special thanks to my ever patient and encouraging wife, Geralyn. It is our prayer that the story of William and Johanna Anderson will inspire all who read it and that it will bless South Africa and her many peoples.

— **Peter S. Anderson**, *1995, Hong Kong*

Preface To The Second Edition

The response from readers to the first edition of "Weapons of Peace" has been incredibly gratifying and humbling. It is my prayer that this second edition will prove to be a blessing to many more readers, – young and old.

Having a second edition has given me the opportunity to make some revisions and corrections, enlarge the page and font size, and include references and an index. References marked CWM/LMS come, of course, from the Council for World Mission (formerly London Missionary Society) archives housed in the library of London University's School of Oriental and African Studies. History is clearly far more gripping than fiction, and history can teach us many important lessons.

I would like to thank Alison Shortridge of Cape Town for her painstaking editing work, picking up many typos missed in the first edition. I am also very grateful to Dr Charles Helm of Canada, like me a descendant of William and Johanna Anderson, who provided me with some very helpful additional material.

Zorko Sostaric, a GIS mapping professional with Eagle Technology Group in Auckland, helped me re-do the maps, which I think look really great. I am also deeply grateful to Leslie Koh, a professional editor serving with Our Daily Bread Ministries in Singapore, who went through the revised manuscript and made many excellent suggestions. His detailed and expert editing work has greatly improved this edition. Thank you, Leslie – what you did was amazing!

I am indebted to those who have kindly given their commendations – adding to the wonderful foreword written back in 1995 by Michael Cassidy. Thanks too to Our Daily Bread Ministries for their help in getting the second edition to the printers. Having been asked, let me confess – the line drawings at the start of each chapter were done by me. The cover painting for the original edition was done by my Chinese friend, Zhang Yu.

Finally, in my original preface I mentioned the support of "my ever patient and encouraging wife, Geralyn." Geralyn was called home to heaven in 1998 following a battle with cancer. She was only forty-seven. For me it was a huge loss. Since then, however, God has blessed me with a "second blessing" – Elizabeth, who has also been a most wonderful support and encouragement.

— **Peter S. Anderson**, *2015, Auckland*

Cover Painting of First Edition

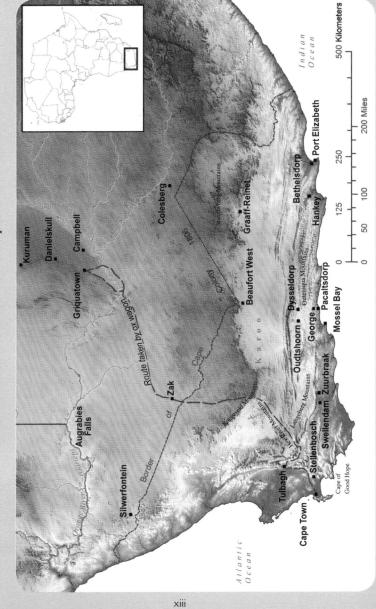

Places Mentioned in "Weapons of Peace"

Settlements North of The Orange River, 1815

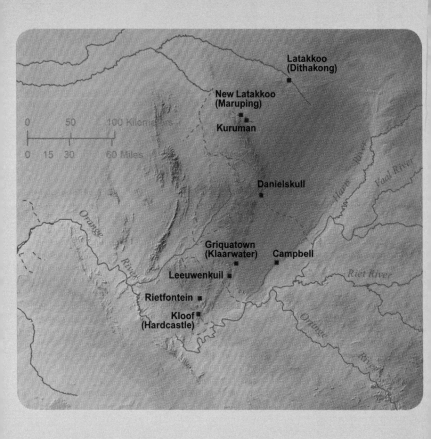

The Story of William & Johanna Anderson

CHAPTER 1:

Africa At Last

$\mathscr{I}$t was a magnificent sight. Though still in the distance and covered with a layer of cloud, the mountain was already dominating the horizon. The early morning air was fresh, and the sea pleasingly calm despite the bracing breeze.

William Anderson and his three companions stood together at the foredeck rail drinking in the beauty. With William were Englishman James Read, and Dutchmen Bastian Tromp and Aart Antony van der Lingen. William, though born in London, prided himself on being a Scot.

It had been a long and at times hazardous voyage. Five months had passed since they said their hurried farewells in London and, on 10 April 1800, set sail for the Cape.[1] It would be wonderful to stand on 'terra firma' again, even if that land was a strange and foreign shore. The Cape of Good Hope, which sometimes lived up to its other name – the Cape of Storms – looked full of exciting promise.

William's mind went back to the memorable meetings of September 1795 in London, when thousands had gathered from all over England and Scotland for the founding of the London Missionary Society – its "sole object to spread the knowledge of Christ among the heathen and other unenlightened nations".

William had been at those meetings and had wanted to offer his services to the newly formed Society.

At the time he was only twenty-five and had, since his father's death in 1789, been running the family business. His father, also a William, had as a young man come to London from Aberdeen in Scotland, and set himself up as a silk merchant. It was in London that the elder William met and married Catherine Turner from Devon.

The younger William was their oldest child. Two younger boys and a girl had died when in their teens, and after his father's death, William felt the responsibility, not only of the business, but also of looking after his mother and two remaining brothers, Edward and John. Tragically, two years after the elder William's passing, John also died at the age of sixteen.

Though eager to serve in the LMS, William knew his mother needed him. So he took care of her until she too passed away in March 1797. Both William's parents had been active 'non-comformists' – evangelicals who preferred to remain outside the state church. William buried his mother beside his father in the 'non-conformist' graveyard of Bunhill Fields, in London's east-end. Barely five months later, his one remaining brother, Edward, also died at twenty-six, leaving William without any immediate family. It made him all the more firmly convinced that God was calling him to serve overseas, and willing to go anywhere the LMS sent him.

It was decided that William would be part of the second group being sent to the Cape. He had already been reading all he could lay his hands on concerning Africa and other areas of interest to the LMS. William was also keenly interested in the work in India of William Carey, the Baptist.

Having prepared for so long, William could never have imagined his actual departure for Africa would be so sudden. As it turned out, he and the other three were only given twenty-four hours' notice for their final packing. He hardly had time

2

to say good-bye. He knew he might never see his friends and supporters again.

A large group of friends gathered at the dockside to wave him off. Among them was a beautiful young lady from a wealthy London home. She was, like William, an active Christian, and he would have happily proposed marriage to her, but he knew she was not prepared to follow him overseas into the unknown. She admired him but did not feel 'called' in the same way. Just thinking about all this brought a lump to William's throat.

The Europe that William left behind in 1800 was in political and social upheaval. England and France were at war, Napoleon Bonaparte was a name to be feared, and even on the high seas William and his companions had not been able to escape the realities of the conflict.

Not long after leaving English shores, their ship had encountered a French privateer that engaged them in a fierce battle of cannon fire. It was a chilling experience, not least for James Read, who still had vivid memories of his last encounter with a French warship.

Read had been in an earlier group of missionaries on board a ship called 'The Duff' which, while en-route for Tahiti, had been seized first by a French privateer and then by the Portuguese. He had been imprisoned in Lisbon before eventually being shipped back to England. Read, however, had a strong sense of adventure and an even stronger personality. His stubborn will was both a strength and a potential weakness. Even war in Europe would not stop James Read in his determination to travel overseas again. On this second voyage the captain of their vessel had out-fought the French and captured the captain of the privateer.

Now they were approaching Cape Town, and all the drama of the voyage was behind them. William had been so completely lost in his thoughts that he was startled when Read suddenly slapped his shoulder, exclaiming,

"Look at those dolphins, William!" A pod of dolphins were playfully diving in and out of the gentle waves.

William was excited. At thirty, he was about to embark on a new and unknown life. Shielding his eyes from the sun, he peered towards land, then turned to James Read.

"A safer voyage than your last one, James, but we had our anxious moments, didn't we? Only the Almighty knows what lies before us."

William sensed that here in Africa, great events were unfolding. Soon, he and his companions would be plunged into a turmoil of clashing cultures and peoples.

All four of them became silent, captivated by the sheer beauty of the scene before them. The precipitous sides of the mountain rose majestically from the ocean. Flat on the top with its white 'table-cloth' of cloud under a blue sky, William could see why it was called Table Mountain. To the left was the jagged Devil's Peak and to the right, a slightly lower peak called Lion's Head. They could see the full sweep of Table Bay, and as they came closer, the main settlement at the Cape came into view.

Cape Town, or De Kaap, backed by the imposing vertical ramparts of Table Mountain, was a small cluster of buildings that fronted onto the sea and extended a little way up the lower slopes of Lion's Head.

Their eyes now glued on the settlement, the four men could make out the Castle, a fort built in the seventeenth century by the Dutch East India Company, and several other large buildings, which included the Barracks, the Burgher Senate House and the Dutch Church.

A long wooden jetty, locally known as the 'Jutty', extended from close to the Castle about a hundred metres out into the bay. It was the only safe landing place and thronged with people. A large crowd had gathered for the arrival of the ship.

4

Amid much shouting and rope throwing the ship was finally secured to large wooden stakes on the 'Jutty', and the gangplank was lowered. Along with other luggage-laden passengers, soldiers, sailors and prisoners, including the captain of the French privateer, William and his companions stumbled their way down onto the 'Jutty'.

"Welkom, Welkom!" came the warm greeting.

Among the crowd, and obviously glad to see them, were local friends and directors of the South African Missionary Society (SA Society). The SA Society had been formed the previous year following the arrival of the first LMS missionary to Africa, Dr Johannes T. van der Kemp.

"The Society wrote from London and told us of your coming," said Mr Ledeboer,[2] one of the directors of the SA Society, as he grasped their hands in delight. "We've been expecting you for a couple of months."

Bartholomeus Schonken, a local official and also one of the directors of the SA Society, added,

"You will be ready for a good meal. My wife and daughters have been busy preparing."

By then it was quite late in the afternoon, and William and his companions were very grateful for the warm welcome and the promise of hospitality. Their heavy bags and boxes were loaded on to horse wagons waiting in a nearby open square called the Parade.

William looked around fascinated. Cape Town was a neat town with houses of brick faced with stucco of lime. Many had a raised platform in the front, called a 'stoep'. There were some twenty or so streets intersecting at right angles, none of them paved. Oak or pinaster trees had been planted at intervals on either side of the streets.

"They is called Heerengracht and Keizersgracht[3]," said Mr Schonken, pointing out the two main streets in his broken

English. William wondered if he would ever get his tongue around those two names.

"You see them lodging houses and canteens, they is mostly for the use of sailors passing at the Cape," Schonken continued. "Too much drinking and other nonsense, I'm afraid. Not surprising they call De Kaap the 'Tavern of the Seas'."

Cape Town in 1800 had a population of close to 50,000, of whom about 22,000 were European colonists.[4] Though used to cosmopolitan London, William was still amazed at the different kinds of people he saw.

There were well-dressed Europeans who could have come straight from London or Rotterdam. There were, he noticed, with not a little delight, Scotsmen in green and black kilts – members of the Argyllshire Highlanders. In the spring of 1795, the Highlanders had ended the Dutch East India Company's long rule at the Cape when they defeated Commissioner-General Sluysken and his half-hearted defence. The Highlanders were now part of the British garrison occupying the Castle.

William also noticed the burghers, some on horseback, local citizens who had taken to farming. Most were from wine or wheat farms within a fifty mile radius of Cape Town.[5]

There were also tough-looking, sun-tanned Colonists who appeared to have a different air about them. Mr Schonken explained they were the semi-nomadic trekboers who normally roamed about the interior with their cattle and were happiest when far from any authority.

"They is come to De Kaap to sell their beasts and buy in market," he said.

Realising that Mr Schonken was happier speaking in Dutch, William apologised for having little understanding of the language.

"I did learn a little from brothers Tromp and van der Lingen while on the voyage," he said, well aware even from the brief time since his arrival that he was not going to hear much English spoken in the Cape.

Even more interesting to William were the darker faces among the crowds. There were handsome-looking Malay slaves with long black shiny hair. Some were quite fair in complexion, and some of the Malay women were strikingly beautiful. The much darker men, William was told, were mostly from Mozambique or Madagascar. He was grieved to hear that all of them were slaves.

Mr Schonken explained,

"The poor slaves is more than all the Europeans in De Kaap."[6]

"When will such evils be no more?" William asked.

Mr Schonken said nothing but nodded as if he felt the same way.

Someone William greatly admired back in London was Member of Parliament, William Wilberforce. Wilberforce and others had for some years been fighting the slave trade.

Another distinct group of people caught William's attention. They were the "yellow-skinned" Khoikhoi, commonly called Hottentots by the white Colonists. The original inhabitants of the Cape, they had at one time, been the main suppliers of cattle for passing ships and for the early Dutch settlers. However in the Cape, Khoikhoi clan structures and organisation were no more. Almost a century earlier, many of them had been wiped out through a smallpox epidemic.

Most surviving Khoikhoi in the area of De Kaap, and in the fertile valleys and coastal mountains across the wind-blown Cape Flats, had drifted into service with former employees of the now-defunct Dutch East India Company or with the burghers.[7] But there were still many Khoikhoi clans living to the north of the areas settled by the Colonists. Many had retreated inland away from the encroaching white man.

The horse wagons were loaded and the four newly arrived missionaries and their welcoming party set off. After a short sight-seeing ride through the streets of the town, they took the main road past the Castle and out through a gate which was normally closed after dark.

In less than twenty minutes, they arrived at the home of Mr and Mrs Schonken in a little village called Salt River. As they alighted, they could see, across an open space, three ox-wagons being out-spanned for the night, as one by one the oxen were unhitched from the wagons.

"The burghers usually rest here after their journey and first thing in the morning go to the market in De Kaap," explained Mr Ledeboer.

The sun was setting and the sky was a breath-taking blaze of colour. Devil's Peak was a brooding silhouetted shadow.

Soon all the men were enjoying a delicious meal of mutton cooked by the cheerful Mrs Schonken and her two daughters Johanna and Maria. The Schonkens were descendants of some of the earliest Dutch and French Huguenot settlers in the Cape. The Huguenots had arrived in 1688 after fleeing the religious persecutions of that time in Europe.[8]

That night, William knelt beside his bed to pray. As his mind flashed back over the events of the day, he found himself full of praise to God. It was a day he would never forget. So many compelling images, both of the people and the scenery, had etched themselves in his mind.

For a moment, he found himself thinking about twenty-four-year-old Johanna Schonken and her friendly smile.

"She is pretty," he thought to himself, "and seems a good lass all right!"

Soon, however, his mind turned to the significance of his arrival at long last in Africa. He knew God wanted him here, and wondered what exciting adventures, or dangers, awaited him. He committed his future to God, and finally pulled himself onto the bed. It was not long before he sank into deep sleep.

[1] Lovett, Richard: The History of the London Missionary Society, 1795-1895, Volume 1, Oxford University Press, 1899, p 522.

[2] SOAS, CWM/LMS Archives, Jan 27,1800, Letter from Dr T Haweis to Mr Ledeboer.

[3] Present-day Adderley and Darling Streets.

[4] le Cordeur, Basil A: The Occupations of the Cape, 1795-1854, from An Illustrated History of South Africa, Jonathan Ball Publishers, Johannesburg 1986, p75.

[5] Pollock & Agnew: An Historical Geography of South Africa, Longmans, London, 1963, p100.

[6] 1798 Census - 21,746 European colonists, 25,000 slaves.

[7] Boucher, Maurice: The Cape under the Dutch East India Company, chapter 5 of An Illustrated History of South Africa, Jonathan Ball Publishers, Johannesburg 1986, pp.70-72.

[8] The Huguenots arrived in the Cape just thirty-five years after the arrival, in 1652, of a group of ninety men, women and children led by Jan van Riebeeck of the Dutch East India Company.

CHAPTER 2.

Decision Made

*W*illiam woke early. He pushed open the green shutters and what he saw almost took his breath away.

The rays of the early morning sun were just touching the east-facing ridges of Devil's Peak and Table Mountain. The sight reminded him of the greatness and unchanging faithfulness of the Creator.

"What a sight!" he thought to himself.

The breakfast bell rang and the Schonkens and their guests sat down around the large wooden table. Mr Schonken read from a Dutch Bible before offering a simple prayer. The women served strong coffee and freshly baked bread. There was a choice of honey, homemade marmalade or melon and ginger jam.

"William, tell us about your family," Mr Schonken said. "What does your father do? Is he in good health?"

"My parents have both passed away, sir," replied William.

"I am sorry, William," said Mr Schonken, a little embarrassed. William sensed that he was not just being polite, but was genuinely interested in his background.

"My father was a merchant in London, and from my late teen years I assisted my father in his business, " William continued.

"My parents were both active Christians but at the time I was not too interested in religion."

"When did you become interested then, William?" asked Mr Schonken.

"It all goes back to when, as a young teenager, I heard John Wesley preaching. He was an old man by then but still preached with great power."

Mr Schonken leaned forward. He had heard much about the great English preachers, John Wesley and George Whitfield.

"They say Wesley and Whitfield did save England from revolution," he said.

"They certainly made a deep impact in England," agreed William. "The spiritual revolution in my country has brought renewal and wholeness to both society and the churches."

"So then, did listening to Wesley preach bring you to personal faith, William?" asked Mr Schonken.

"Surprisingly, perhaps – no, it did not. At the time, despite hearing Mr Wesley, I resisted the gospel, even though I knew it to be true."

"What made you come to Africa as a missionary then, Mr Anderson?" Johanna asked shyly. She had been trying not to show too much interest, but had in fact been listening closely.

"It was about seven years ago when William Carey went to India, that I began to realise how empty my own religion was – at best it was second-hand," said William. "Carey's example stirred me deeply and my own life began to take on new meaning and direction. I felt God was also calling me to serve Him overseas."

"However, I promised my father before he died that I would look after my mother. She herself was not well and needed special care. Only after Mother died about three years ago did I feel free to offer myself to the Society."

The Schonkens were moved by William's affection for his parents. The Dutch traditionally laid great stress on family ties.

"I will tell you about our family some time," whispered Johanna as they got up from the table.

"I would like that," replied William.

Huguenot Jean Prieur Du Plessis, one of Johanna's forebears came to Africa over one hundred years prior to William's arrival.

The next day, the SA Society held an important meeting during which its directors met with the four newly arrived recruits. They were joined by John Kicherer who happened to be visiting Cape Town. He had been in the first party of missionaries sent by the LMS the previous year, and had been working for several months among the San people – commonly called Bushmen – north of the Cape mountains in the dry interior at a place called the Zak River.

Dr Haweis, one of the founding directors of the LMS and a renowned minister in London, had asked the SA Society to take responsibility for the deployment of the latest recruits.[9] In his letter to the directors of the SA Society Dr Haweis wrote, "The LMS has full confidence in our Dutch Brethren and we feel you are best able to make wise decisions according to local conditions." The LMS was grateful for the enthusiastic help that the first group of missionaries led by Dr van der Kemp had received.[10]

One of the local directors, Manenberg, called the meeting to order. "A hearty welcome to our new friends from England and Holland, and also to Brother Kicherer."

"Many exciting things are happening," he continued. "We have received news that Dr van der Kemp, who is now residing among the Xhosa people beyond the eastern border of the Colony, has already met the Xhosa chief Ngqika and preached the gospel to him."[11]

The significance of this news was not missed by those gathered. The black peoples of southern Africa, so numerous in areas to the east of the European settlements in the south west and southern Cape, could not be ignored. They may have been seen by the Colonists as a barrier to further settlement, and conflict with them may have seemed inevitable. To the missionary, however, they were people who needed to hear the 'Good News'.

The likes of Dr van der Kemp were often misunderstood, criticised, and even despised, by fellow whites. Few realised the importance of mutual respect, rather than paternalism, in fostering peace and understanding between the different and competing cultures in southern Africa. Most missionaries, however, sought to identify with the indigenous peoples by learning their language and by giving of themselves in practical service. They believed in living out the gospel they preached.

Reports were given about the situation in the Cape and about the different groups of people living inland and to the east.

James Read and Aart van der Lingen were already determined to join Dr van der Kemp in his work among the Xhosa. William was still considering his options and he listened with special interest to Kicherer's report. Though working mainly amongst the San, Kicherer referred several times to a group of Khoikhoi known as the Korana. Kicherer also spoke of two colleagues, William Edwards from England and Cornelius Kramer who was from the Cape. Kramer was the first locally-born missionary to be sent out by the fledgling SA Society.

"Perhaps Kramer is Africa's first home-grown missionary", thought William. He knew about the work done by the German Moravian, George Schmidt, following his arrival in the Cape in 1737, but attempts by Dutch settlers themselves to evangelize the Khoikhoi had been few and far between.

After lunch William spoke at length with Kicherer and asked him to tell him more about the San and the Korana.

"The Bushmen normally roam about in small bands," said Kicherer, using the common term for the San. "They are hunters and also live off roots, berries and fruits that the women collect. They are small of stature and to us seem very primitive."

"Are they dangerous or warlike?"

"They are very savage at times and their poisoned arrows are deadly. It has been known for people to pass within a few yards of them and never know they were there – they keep so silent and still. They are brilliant trackers and 'read' signs in the ground knowing what kind of animal has passed by and when."

"What about their language?" asked William with interest. "Can you speak much yet?"

Kicherer shook his head, and replied with obvious resignation,

"It's beyond me! Their language contains four or even five different click sounds.[12] I haven't made much progress in mastering the language yet."

Kicherer also shared about the San's religious beliefs, which included a deep fear of the supernatural and of evil spirits.

"I know that our 'mission' is not to impose our culture upon these so-called 'primitive' peoples," said William, "but surely they too deserve the chance to hear about Christ."

He had a strong impression that though they were well-adapted to their environment, the San often lived in far from ideal conditions and were a people for whom life itself was a struggle.

William also wanted to know more about the Korana. "Are the Korana anything like the Khoikhoi here in the Cape? What languages do they speak?" he asked.

Kicherer said he knew less about the Korana than he did about the San. "From what I do know, it seems the Korana are a branch or tribe of the Khoikhoi. They are also hunters, like the Bushmen, but seem to depend far more on their herds of cattle. Significant numbers of Korana, I have been told, live beyond the boundaries of the Colony, along the Orange River."

"Have you been anywhere near the Orange River?" asked William.

"Few whites have even seen the Orange River. None has resided anywhere near it," Kicherer replied. He was warming to William for showing such interest in his work. "Some of the Korana near us have talked of the River. It is many hundreds of miles and several weeks travel further north even from the Zak."

William found himself strangely drawn to these peoples.

Over the next few weeks William had the opportunity to explore the area around Cape Town. He noticed the incredible variety of plants and flowers. Here in the south-western corner of Africa, with its winter rainfall and convoluted fold mountains, was a diversity of plant life and flora unsurpassed in the world, with many thousands of indigenous species. The slopes of Table Mountain were covered with heath-land vegetation, called 'fynbos' by the locals, meaning 'fine bush' – a rich hue of purple, mauve, yellow and green.

Further round Table Mountain from Salt River were the growing settlements of Rondebosch and Wynberg, with some large and prosperous looking farms. Further east, across the wind-blown sandy Cape Flats were the Cape fold mountains.

"Those mountains are called the Hottentots Holland Mountains," Johanna Schonken told William. It was in the fertile valleys nestled up against those mountains that her ancestors from Holland and France had first settled.

It was not always easy for William to understand all that was being said. His new friends, including the Schonken family, conversed at great speed in Dutch.

"Many of these Colonists have strange accents, but you'll get used to it," whispered van der Lingen. "Those of us from Holland speak a purer Dutch."

"Accent or no accent, I surely hope to learn as much as my old brain can absorb," replied William. "I hope I can learn some Bushman and some Korana too."

William enjoyed learning all he could about the area around the Cape. Yet his mind was increasingly pre-occupied with thoughts about his future work somewhere inland, beyond the distant Hottentots Holland Mountains.

The directors were not in a hurry. They wanted to be sure of God's leading before making any decisions. Finally, they decided that James Read should – as he had wished – join Dr van der Kemp among the Xhosa. William was to join Kicherer, Edwards and Kramer at the Zak River.[13] But first, he would spend a few months learning Dutch and acquainting himself with the Korana. William's first five months passed quickly.

Early in the morning of 10 February, 1801, he and Kicherer bid farewell to the crowd of well-wishers who had gathered to see them off. As he said a brief and what appeared to be an ordinary good-bye to Johanna Schonken, William found his heart beating faster.

"It might not be a very spiritual reason," he thought, "but I really want to learn to speak Dutch well so that I can impress Johanna." He prayed a silent prayer, "Dear God, please bless Johanna and her family. I think I'll miss them, especially Johanna."

Unknown to him, Johanna too had a little prayer. "Lord, do protect Mr Anderson and please may we meet again," she whispered as the ox-wagon carrying William and Kicherer disappeared into the distance.

---

[9] SOAS,CWM/LMS Archives, CWM/LMS/05/02/02, Haweis to Ledeboer, Jan 27, 1800.

[10] Ibid

[11] John Theodosius Van Der Kemp Papers, CWM/LMS/20/02/12

[12] Marshall, Lorna: The Kung of Nyae Nyae, Cambridge, Mass., Harvard University Press, 1976.

[13] CWM/LMS/05/02/02/005/005, Letter stating approval of decision, LMS to SA Society, Oct 1801

CHAPTER 3:

With The Korana

The journey over the mountains and through the valleys of the south western Cape took William through some of Africa's most magnificent scenery. Rugged sandstone peaks towered above them, while the rock-strewn slopes were covered with all kinds of flower-sprouting bushes and fynbos. At night they camped beside crystal-clear streams under the myriads of stars lavishly spilled across the southern sky's Milky Way. The further they went inland, the less hospitable the mountains became. There were no proper trails and some of the passes were little more than rough tracks. Once they were north of the forbidding Roggeveld mountains, however, the terrain became noticeably drier. The vegetation consisted mainly of small clumpy bushes. The days were hot, but the nights pleasantly cool.

"Not much to see now," Kicherer said to William as they covered mile after mile of dry, open space, "but I tell you, you should see it in the early spring. After just a few showers, the whole place, as far as the eye can see, is ablaze with colour. It is literally a carpet of flowers."

Several times they saw huge herds of springbok grazing peacefully. As the travellers approached, the graceful animals would raise their proud horns and then, at some secret signal, the whole herd would suddenly take flight. It was an awesome sight as tens of thousands of animals, with great leaps and bounds, took to their heels.

Five weeks after setting out from Cape Town, William and Kicherer finally arrived at the small 'mission-station' at Zak River, where they received a warm welcome from Edwards, Kramer and the local San and Khoikhoi.

William was fascinated by all he saw, especially the local people. All that Kicherer had told him about the San seemed so much more real as he mixed with these small but friendly people.

Before long, however, he discovered, to his great disappointment, that Edwards and Kicherer did not get on too happily.[14] Edwards was critical of Kicherer, and told William that Kicherer was too slack in his 'Sabbath keeping'. While William had been brought up in a strict moral and religious environment and had strong convictions about what was right and wrong, he sensed Edwards was being too much of a legalist.

At heart, William was a peace-maker.

"Brother Edwards," he pleaded, "I urge you to act in accordance with the Bible's admonitions. If you feel Brother Kicherer has a fault, you should approach him about it in love and humility."

"I've lived and worked with the man. He would not take my advice," Edwards snorted impatiently.

It grieved William that such a petty problem could cause conflict between Christian brothers. "O Lord," he prayed, "what weak and sinful creatures we are! How can we ever be of use to you in touching the hearts of the heathen when our own hearts so need your touch?"

Edward's feelings were, partly at least, the result of the difficulties he faced in coping with a new and arduous environment, which aggravated the cultural differences between the two men. Kicherer was from Holland and Edwards from England. They had different backgrounds, values and perceptions of things such as 'Sabbath observance'.

A few weeks later, it was decided that William would take a trip further north, possibly as far as the Orange River. He was eager to find out more about the peoples living there, and was also glad to be out on his own – and to get away from the conflict between Edwards and Kicherer. William hated conflict.

With a wagon full of supplies, as well as several sheep and cattle, he set off, accompanied by a group of 'mixed breed Hottentots' who were known by the unhappy term 'Bastards'. It was only twelve years later that they would adopt the name Griqua, a name derived from the Grigriqua, the original Khoikhoi clan from which some of their more influential families were descended.[15]

Though largely of Khoikhoi origin, the Griqua also had some white ancestry. Quite a number of them had a European father or grandfather, or San parents. Most had Dutch names and spoke a corruption of Dutch that incorporated words from the Khoikhoi and San languages. They were thus adept at communicating with San, Korana and Nama peoples.

Most of the Griqua living within the borders of the Colony wore European clothes; some were even land-owners. In many ways they were not very different to the white trekboers who roamed about with their cattle in the interior. Life was cheap. Guns and gun-powder were essential for hunting as well as protection from both man and wild animals. The Griqua travelling with William knew the country well, and they also knew some of the people living along the Orange River.

"It is a very dangerous journey. Many Bushmen, dangerous," warned one of them. The others nodded.

Though William and his colleagues prayed to God for a safe journey before he set out, the Griqua felt more inclined to rely on their weapons than on the missionaries' God. Many of them knew about God, especially those who had had close contact with burghers or trekboers. Most of the Colonists were, nominally at least, staunch Calvinists who held uncompromisingly to strict, conservative Protestant traditions. It was their daily custom to gather their families and servants for prayer and a reading from the Dutch Bible.

Much of the country north of the Zak River was dry and barren. The vast expanse was broken occasionally by massive flat-topped hills with almost-vertical sides, and a lot of it rocky, home to little more than the occasional bush. In some parts there was plenty of grass and a great variety of game, in even greater numbers than those William had seen earlier. His Griqua travelling companions were only too happy to tell him the names of the animals in Dutch, and sometimes in Korana or San. They included eland, wildebeest, springbok, buffalo, zebra, ostriches and occasionally, giraffe. There were great herds of quagga, which were similar to zebra except that they had stripes only on the head and neck.[16]

"Quagga are easy to hunt and they are good for eating," the men told William.

None of them would have known that on account of excessive hunting the quagga many years later became extinct.

The journey had been going well until one day towards evening, when William noticed that they were being followed. On a slight ridge to their left, he caught sight of a few figures, crouching and running. He soon realised that there were others to their right as well. They were being shadowed by a fairly large number of San, all armed with bows and arrows.

"Not good," said one of the Griqua men, "the Bushmen want to steal and maybe kill."

William felt a little apprehensive as his party made camp that night. Despite their guns, the men seemed more than happy to join him as he prayed to God for protection. They slept with loaded guns by their side.

When he awoke in the faint light of early morning, William noticed the San were still there. If they had any intent on doing harm, however, they were clearly in no hurry to act. William prayed out loud, thanking God for His protection. The San disappeared shortly afterwards, as suddenly as they had appeared. It was not the last time on that trip that William saw San.

In the afternoon of 5 April 1801, they reached the green, wooded valley of the Orange River. Some of the trees were of a considerable height, towering twenty or even thirty metres above them.[17] In his broken Dutch, a delighted William told the men,

"Beautiful, it is very pretty here. This is surely the most pleasant part of Africa I have seen!" They nodded.

The flow of the Orange River was particularly strong where the valley was narrower and where the banks were steep. At other places it was much broader perhaps five or even 600 yards wide, William estimated, and seemed more sluggish.

"Certainly twice the width of the Thames at high tide," he thought. "London, my, but that seems far away!" He had a twinge of home sickness, but it did not last long. Everything was so interesting, and he was getting to know and enjoy being with his Griqua companions.

The men told him that during the four or five months when the rains came, the river was even fuller and was difficult to cross. At other times it was easy to wade through.

The next day, they tied pieces of timber together to make floats, which were used to get the wagon and themselves across the river. Most of the cattle and sheep were swum across. By then it was about midday. They had hardly had time to dry off when William was startled by a sudden commotion.

The strangest sight confronted him. A great number of huge, bulky creatures, which William called 'sea horses', were thrashing about in the water. They had massive jaws which could open to an unbelievable size. They were the first hippos he had seen.

It was common to hear lions at night, and from time to time leopards also would attack and kill unprotected cattle or sheep.

William also began to meet large numbers of Korana[18] who lived in small kraals, or villages, scattered along the banks of the Orange River. Their dwellings were small, spherical huts consisting of curved wooden frames covered with mats made of woven grass or reed. They slept on skins or reed mats. To scoop or hold water they used containers cut out of wood or made from hollowed out calabashes.

The Korana could strike village and move within half an hour. The staves and mats, as well as their utensils, could be packed onto the backs of their docile oxen, and off they would go to set up somewhere else.

William was amazed at the way they handled their oxen. They seemed to treat them with great care, even affection. According to the Griqua, the Korana were unequalled when it came to training and riding oxen. They fastened a bridle to a wooden pin struck through the ox's nose, and used a piece of sheepskin as a saddle.

William was not too sure he wanted to try riding the oxen, but with the encouragement of both the Griqua and the Korana, he eventually did. The crowd of bemused onlookers burst into spontaneous applause when William finally managed, after three or four embarrassing attempts, to stay astride the objecting ox. Almost more than anything else he did, this little action endeared him to the Korana.

The people wore hardly any clothing. The men sported a small frontal covering of tanned skin made from the hide of cattle or antelope, while the women wore a skirt-like covering of skin attached around their waist. In colder weather, both men and women would wrap a large skin, or kaross, around themselves.

William enjoyed the company of these easygoing, friendly people. They looked like most of the Khoikhoi he had met, but had less prominent cheekbones and more oval-looking faces. He couldn't help laughing sometimes – to himself of course – when he saw the men riding their oxen in great ceremony and the women running after them.

What William never got used to was the way the Korana and some of his Griqua companions ate after they had been on a hunt. The animals were roasted over a fire, and both men and women would devour, at great speed, huge volumes of meat. One man could, by himself, finish an entire sheep in one sitting. Their stomachs would distend so much that William imagined they might burst at any moment. The San, too, could devour unbelievable quantities of meat. At the same time all of them could also go without food – and sometimes did – for days on end.

More than three months had passed since William had said good-bye to his colleagues at the Zak River; the time had just flown by. He was enjoying living with the Korana, and his Griqua friends helped him communicate with them when his sign language got him nowhere. One or two of the Korana even understood some Dutch. Mutual friendships developed, and the Korana began to show interest in William's God.

"We don't know about your God. You can come and live with us and teach us," one of their leaders told him.

"I would love to do that," William replied excitedly. then he added, almost as an after-thought, "If I came, would you consider staying in one place and would you begin planting crops?"

The Korana simply laughed. One of the men told the others in their own language, "This white man is a good man.

He is different from most we have heard about, but he doesn't understand us. Not yet!"

---

[14] CWM/LMS/05/02/02 Incoming Correspondence

[15] Legassick, Martin C: The Griqu, The Sotho-Tswana and the Missionaries, 1780-1840: The Politics of a Frontier Zone, PhD dissertation, University of California, Los Angeles, 1969.

[16] Skinner, J. D.; Chimimba, C. T: The Mammals of the Southern African Sub-region (3rd ed.), Cambridge University Press, Cambridge, 2005, pp. 537–546.

[17] CWM/LMS/05/02/02, Anderson to LMS, Dec 6, 1801.

[18] Bredekamp, H.C.: The Origin of the Southern African Khoisan Communities, from An Illustrated History of South Africa, Jonathan Ball Publishers, Johannesburg 1986, pp.28-30.

CHAPTER 4:

Danger Unawares

The weather was much colder, especially at night, and William joined the Korana around their fires in the evening. Each man carried a knife in a small leather case slung around his neck, along with another small bag or tortoise shell in which he kept a pipe, some tobacco and a flint stone. The men often lit up as they sat huddled around the fire.

Occasionally, William would hear the plaintive sounds of the ancient Khoikhoi musical instrument, the t'Gorrah, floating eerily in the night air. The t'Gorrah consisted of a curved piece of wood over which a long single string of catgut was stretched. A quill was attached at one end, and blowing on this made the catgut vibrate, producing a variety of sounds.[19] William watched in fascination one evening as an old man, lying on his side with one ear to the ground, played the instrument.

"I could get to like this music," he thought.

At the Orange, William met many more Griqua. He heard about some famous Griqua chiefs – or captains as they were called – who owned large herds of cattle and flocks of sheep.

One of the richest was Cornelius Kok; another leading family clan were the Berends. William was to get to know them well.

Scattered along the Orange River, were many communities, sometimes mixed, of Griqua, Korana, and Namaqua. To the north and north-east were large numbers of black peoples collectively called the Tswana. The San lived in villages, mostly to the south of the River.

It was soon obvious to William that the Griqua and Korana treated the San with total contempt. In fact, their attitudes were not much different from those of some burghers in the Colony who thought little of organising commandos to exterminate the San. Despite this, the richer Griqua sometimes had San servants and even concubines.

It was a bitterly cold morning on 8 July but the warm sunshine soon brightened William's spirits. Around midday two wagons approached, and William was overjoyed to see Kicherer and Kramer, who had travelled up from the Zak to find out how he was doing. With them was Schols, a traveller from the Cape who was exploring the interior.

William asked how Edwards was doing, only to be told that, sadly the LMS had severed links with him, and the Englishman had decided to go off on his own.[20] William was disappointed, but not surprised.

After consulting the Korana leaders, William and his colleagues decided to move north to a place called Rietfontein, meaning Reed Fountain. It was three days' travel away and lay several kilometres from the Orange River, but seemed a good place for planting a garden. It had a natural spring.

There, they built a large house of reeds which doubled as a simple church that could hold up to 400 people. William soon felt at home. The missionaries began to teach the people – of whom there were several hundred, mostly Korana – in the immediate vicinity.[21]

William could hardly believe what he was seeing. A crowd of 300, or on occasion as many as 600, listened with rapt attention as he and his colleagues took turns to tell the Korana of God's love. For most of them, if not all, it was the first time they had heard the name of Jesus. Many shed tears as they listened.

William was himself gripped afresh by the wonder of the message he shared that the Sovereign God loved all men, including these semi-nomadic Korana, Namaqua, Griqua, and even the despised San.

The method of preaching used by the missionaries was the simple exposition of suitable passages of Scripture. As the people listened, some shook visibly as if convicted by a sense of fear or guilt. At times it was difficult to even continue with the meeting, for there seemed such distress. Some evenings they spoke to the Korana; on other evenings, it would be the turn of the Griqua.[22]

The missionaries preached in Dutch. No one seemed to bother about or even notice William's grammatical mistakes and limited vocabulary, although his Dutch had improved noticeably. When speaking to the Korana, they needed to use interpreters. One young Griqua called Nicholas Bernard translated with great fluency and dramatic effect, even imitating the preacher's actions and facial expressions. Another, called Old Bernard, had more difficulty translating, but appeared to be moved by all he heard. He would sometimes break down as he spoke.

Early each morning, smaller groups would gather for some singing, reading from the Dutch Bible, and a prayer. This was followed by 'school' for those who wished to learn to read. William found the children particularly eager and quick to learn. An average of forty to sixty attended school. When it came to learning, the Griqua appeared more studious than the Korana, owing to the fact that, with Dutch as the medium of instruction, they found it easier. William had only managed to learn a few phrases in Korana. He found the 'tongsmacks', or clicks, almost impossible to master. Kicherer and the others were no better.

By December, Kicherer, who had not been very well, and Schols had left and returned to the Zak. William and Kramer carried on at Rietfontein, enjoying real harmony as they worked together. It was the start of a fruitful partnership.

"Would it not be good if we could establish a permanent base here, Cornelius?" William mused one day as they discussed their work.

"It sure would," replied Kramer, "but I doubt the local economy will allow it. These people seem conditioned to move every few months. With so many animals, they have to move otherwise the grass would soon be exhausted."

William nodded.

Water supply was another crucial issue. If a spring failed or rainfall was inadequate, the people would pack up and move.

"If necessary, I would gladly move about with them," William said. Kramer said he was ready to do the same.

Not long after Kicherer's departure, they had a surprise visit. The head of a very large Griqua kraal, along with several of his leaders came to see them at Rietfontein. These Griqua lived about eight days' further down the Orange River, and wanted William and Kramer to join them to "instruct them in the way of salvation". They seemed sincere, and over the next few months, made more visits to repeat their request.

William and Kramer prayed together about this request, and began to feel it would be right to move. They could always return to Rietfontein from time to time. The Korana there were often on the move anyway.

What they did not know was that one of the reasons for the invitation was that the Griqua chief had had his eye on their wagon and other useful supplies. Murder could wait till a convenient time.

Blissfully ignorant, the two men left Rietfontein on 3 June, 1802. A large group of Griqua came halfway to meet them, and they soon settled happily among them. Including men, women and children, the group numbered almost 800 people. The people soon became attached to their teachers and as promised supplied them with meat and milk. William and Kramer still had the ox and cow, as well as five sheep, that Kicherer had left with them six months earlier.

The Griqua leaders held a secret meeting early one morning. Sitting in a close huddle, they spoke in lowered voices.

"When are we going to kill them?" asked one of the men. "How come you failed last night?"

"It was very strange," replied one of the plotters. "Last night, when the two of us were about to cut their throats, I felt someone, with an unbelievably powerful grip, grab my hand from behind. I couldn't move."

"Ja, me too," added the other, still shaken. "It was eerie. I found a power controlling me. It was as if I was frozen solid."

It was finally decided, strange though these events were, that they would simply have to wait for another opportunity to kill the missionaries.

William and Kramer, meanwhile, continued to sleep peacefully, not knowing anything about their close shave with death.

Occasionally the Griqua moved, and William and Kramer moved with them. They also ate what the people ate. They found themselves dreaming about bread, which they had not seen for almost eight months. In a place called Sand Kraal, where they stayed for several months, William and Kramer tried, without success, to grow some corn.

At Sand Kraal they saw a heart-warming response to their teaching. The school was well attended, and the son of one of the Griqua captains who had plotted to kill them was showing great promise.[23]

31

"I can see real signs of genuine change in some of the people," Kramer said as the two men relaxed after a meal of meat and goat's milk one evening.

"Yes," replied William, "that fellow John Henry, who helps with most of the interpretation when we preach to the Korana, definitely seems to have believed. His wife was telling me that she and her two children can see a change in him." William smiled, then continued, "For the better, of course."

Kramer put his hands behind his head and stretched, "You know," he mused, "I think we could form a church here. Several show all the evidence of divine grace upon them."

With excitement and full of praise, they turned their thoughts into prayer. No sooner had they said "Amen", when Kramer jumped up and said seriously,

"William, I think you should be ordained. Neither of us is anything but a layman. How can we form a church if we can't administer the sacraments?"

In the Dutch church, only ordained clergymen, known as 'dominees', could baptise or officiate at Holy Communion or marry people.

"Why me?" protested William.

Kramer was quick to respond. "Well, you are older for a start and you are already well-trained."

William again protested, "But I refused ordination in England because I felt strongly that God wanted ordinary people to be active in His service. I know that some of our LMS directors also feel that far too much emphasis is put on the clergy."

"That may be," agreed Kramer, "but you should realise that in the Colony, there is probably even more clericalism around. The 'dominee' or 'predikant' is the only one who is allowed to baptise or administer the Lord's Table."

It was a time when churches in England too were debating the issue of the importance of ordination and the service of laymen like William. William, who had been converted in 1794 when in his early twenties, was from a 'free-church' or 'non-conformist' background. He strongly believed that all Christians, whether ordained or not, were of equal status. The LMS, which was supported by various denominations, including the 'established' church in England, had been criticised in some circles for accepting non-ordained men.

The strong emphasis on ordination in certain circles, both in the Cape and in England, annoyed William. He saw it as unbiblical. However, he was not opposed to an ordained ministry, and in fact believed it to be a very holy calling. He was not sure if he was qualified for or worthy of such a 'calling'.

The two men dropped the subject. But their conversation, started something in William's mind and heart. He could not get away from the growing conviction that, for the sake of God's work among these people, of whom he was already very fond, he should seriously consider ordination. Kramer too felt more and more convinced that William should return to the Cape to be ordained. Some of the people were already asking about baptism and wondered why Kicherer at the Zak River could baptise when neither of their teachers could do it.

And so William found himself heading for the Cape. It took him two weeks to get to the Zak, where he enjoyed some discussion and prayer with Kicherer. Kicherer was in full agreement about the proposed ordination. William set off again, while Kicherer said he would follow as soon as he could. Making good time William descended the final pass in just over two weeks. He could see Table Mountain in the far distance.

It was 1 September 1802 when he arrived outside the Schonken home in Salt River. William was excited. He hadn't told anyone why, and none but the most careful observer would have noticed the look between William and Johanna when their eyes met that day. It certainly was one of more than polite formality.

The next two weeks proved to be a very busy and important time for William. He made sure he saw Johanna as often as he could, though it was always in the company of others and always with due decorum. Despite his growing love for Johanna, however, he did not allow himself to be distracted from his commitment to God's call.

His opposition to 'clericalism' had in no way lessened his sense of the seriousness of ordination, and soon he was being formally interviewed by the directors of the SA Society.[24]

"I hope to be able to buy a new wagon and also a horse so that I might more easily travel to visit the villages scattered up and down the Orange River," he said in his report to the directors on what God was doing among the Korana and Griqua.

The directors too had caught something of his excitement and were most interested to hear about his experiences. They questioned him in detail about his beliefs and his reasons for seeking ordination. Mr Schonken later told his wife that the directors had been impressed with William, not least because the interview had been conducted in Dutch.

Johanna and her sister were at the dinner table when their father repeated his comments about William's improved Dutch. The two girls looked at each other and smiled. The younger Maria knew Johanna 'liked' William.

Kicherer arrived on 9 September. The next day William was ordained. Taking part in the ceremony were the President of the SA Society, Mr Manenberg, Mr Schonken, and seven other directors, as well as Kicherer. It was a solemn but moving occasion.[25]

While in Cape Town, William wasted no time in writing letters to the LMS in London as well as to his friends in England. There was so much to report. He had been over-joyed to find letters waiting for him at the Cape. It had been a year and a half since he had heard news from England. Mail from London could take up to ten months to reach the Orange.

On 15 September 1802, William once again set his face towards the distant parts beyond the border of the Colony. This time he found it a lot harder to say good-bye to Johanna, because he did not know when he would see her again.

"I can't possibly expect her, or anyone, to live as I live," he thought to himself. William's chosen life among the Griqua and the Korana was very, very different from life in Cape Town.

---

[19] Burchell, William John: Travels in the Interior of South Africa, 1810-1812, London, 1822, p.458.

[20] CWM/LMS/05/02/005, LMS Director's Letters, Oct, 1801

[21] CWM/LMS/05/02/02/005, Anderson to LMS Dec 6, 1801

[22] Ibid

[23] CWM/LMS/05/02/02/006, SA Society report of interview with Anderson, September 1802

[24] CWM/LMS/05/02/02/006, Anderson to Hardcastle, 19 September 1802.

[25] CWM/LMS/05/02/02/006, SA Society to LMS, 25 September 1802, report of meeting.

CHAPTER 5:

Apprehensive Farewell

*W*hen William left Cape Town following his ordination, he had no idea that the Cape itself was to change hands twice within the next four years. The first of these changes took place early in 1803 when, following the Treaty of Amiens between Britain and France, the British handed the Cape back to the Dutch.[26]

In the period since 1795, the British Military Government had put down at least two rebellions, when the Khoikhoi joined the Xhosa in armed opposition against the colonists. When the Dutch took over, trouble was still seething under the surface.

The Batavian Republic, which ruled the Netherlands and its colonies, sent a top official, Commissioner-General De Mist, to the Cape. With him was Jan Willem Janssens, who was appointed the Military Governor.[27] At first, De Mist was totally opposed to all missionary activity in the Cape. The directors of the SA Society worked hard using their personal influence in an attempt to soften the attitude of the Batavian authorities.

William and Kramer, however, were well outside the borders of the Colony, and were unaware of all these events – and of the rumours that began to circulate about their 'undesirable' activities.

All through 1803 and well into 1804, the two men continued their semi-nomadic existence living and moving about with the Griqua. They were getting to know them well and were learning more and more about the various Griqua families. In the first couple of years, they associated mostly with the Berend brothers and their followers. Later, they were joined by Cornelius Kok and his large group. Both groups were caught in fierce conflict with the powerful and notorious brigand Klaas Afrikaner and his son Jager. Afrikaner and his followers were behind widespread murder and pillage within the borders of the Colony and beyond. Afrikaner had a price on his head.

All this prompted Cornelius Kok and Berend Berends to discuss the need to act in alliance.

"Berend, my comrade, we need to work together or that mad dictator Afrikaner and his son will destroy our peace, kill our children, and steal our wives," Cornelius Kok said. Then he continued, hardly pausing to take a breath, "And I think our having the missionaries Anderson and Kramer living with us may be beneficial."

"I agree with you, Cornelius," replied Berends. "Though we once intended to kill them and take their wagon, we now find they are more use to us alive. At least through them we might have the chance to get more gunpowder and perhaps even guns."

"Guns – yes, it is necessary for our survival to have more guns. Guns for hunting animals and, when threatened, for hunting down our enemies." Cornelius Kok was a shrewd man. Though at times cruel, he was honest enough to admit that the Griqua were not proficient with bows and arrows like the San and Korana, nor with assegais and spears like the Tswana. The Griqua needed guns to maintain their independence.

There had been severe drought and the people, some of whom had large numbers of animals, spread out over a wide area. At times they would move as often as once every three weeks. William and Kramer often split up to travel with different groups. Sometimes, they were separated from each other by as many as three days' journey.

Apart from those at Rietfontein and Sand Kraal, there were several good springs in the vicinity of the Orange River. One of these springs was called Ongeluksfontein, or Misfortune Spring. The Griqua had given it this name after one of them had killed his companion by accidently firing his gun while cleaning it. Another spring was called Leeuwenkuil – the place where a lion had been killed. William would settle there later as the land was fertile and the water supply reliable. It was very close to an even better spring called Klaarwater, or Clear Water.

William and Kramer continued their preaching, as well as teaching those interested in learning to read.

"Friends," William said one day as he sat talking with a group of Griqua men. "As you know, our chief desire is to tell you about God. But we also want to introduce to you the benefits of a more settled life and in particular to teach you the 'art of agriculture.'"

It was something he and Kramer repeated often. By July 1804, they had managed to encourage several people to start preparing the ground for planting.[28]

Some two days' journey to the north lay areas settled by large numbers of Tswana. William and Kramer were surprised to hear that their former colleague Edwards, who had clashed so unhappily with Kicherer, was in the area. He had arrived several months previously with a family from the Cape – Matthias Kok, his wife and their six children. They were trying to do some missionary work among the Tswana, but with little success. William felt apprehensive when he heard that Edwards and the Koks were also involved in hunting and in trading ivory.

"It is one thing to teach the people the benefits of agriculture, but I feel that to engage in hunting and ivory trading will bring only trouble," William told Kramer. "When guns and profit are involved, our message of peace and reconciliation is compromised."

William's words would prove to be prophetic. In South Africa and elsewhere in the world, whenever messengers of the 'gospel of grace' have allowed themselves to become embroiled in activities for personal gain rather than in bringing benefits to those they claim to be serving, they have left behind a legacy of confusion and distrust. Had William known what would result from the activities of Edwards and Kok, he might have been even more adamant.

There was also an outbreak of inter-clan fighting among the Tswana, prompting Edwards to decide to leave for the Cape. Kramer had been travelling in the area with some Griqua, and was with Edwards when he made his decision to leave. Being unwell, Kramer decided to return with Edwards to Ongeluksfontein, where he and William discussed the idea of his returning to the Colony with Edwards.[29]

"I think it's a good idea, Cornelius," said William. "It's been over three years since you were in the Cape, and a break might be good – and," he added with a smile, "you could also get us supplies of flour, tea and coffee."

"Don't tell me," replied Kramer, "I'd give anything for some bread and jam and a cup of coffee!"

They both laughed.

William thought of another good reason for Kramer to visit the Cape. "It will be good for you to visit your family and friends. Many will be wondering if you are still alive."

"And," William added, "I can give you some letters to deliver for me."

Kramer raised his eyebrows and said with a teasing smile,

"Any of them letters for one of the Schonken daughters, by any chance?"

William went a little red. Kramer knew his colleague well enough to know that he thought about Johanna often, even though William saw little hope of them ever being married.

Both men became more serious as Kramer continued,

"My main concern, if I do go, is for your safety. Since those bad characters turned up here, the people have not been as cooperative. I've sensed quite a bit of discontent, and it is not perhaps as safe as it was when we first came to these parts."

Kramer was not referring to Edwards and the Koks. Despite their differences, they were still friends and, to some extent, colleagues. Rather, he was referring to a group of six fugitives who had arrived from the eastern border of the Colony about a month earlier. They had fallen foul of the law, having illegally tried to occupy Xhosa territory.

When the Military Governor Janssens and the Xhosa chief Ngqika made peace, the government had ordered all colonists out of the area.[30] These men and their families had left the Colony in disgust. Two of them, Koenraad Besuitenhout and Kobus Vry, were particularly notorious. They had two wagons and five guns, and soon after arriving at the Orange they helped a group of Korana attack a San village, killing several people and taking their cattle, sheep, and some children. They also got into an ugly dispute with some Griqua after the latter discovered that Besuitenhout had sold them a gun with a faulty lock.[31]

A few days before Kramer returned with Edwards from Tswana country, some of the Griqua men had come to talk to William. They told him about the argument with Besuitenhout and Vry over the faulty gun.

"Mijnheer Anderson, you must help us," one of the men pleaded. "These white men from the colony have threatened to kill us."

William was not eager to pick a fight with the colonists, but knew he could not ignore the appeal of 'his people'.

"It could be dangerous, but let us pray that God will help us," he replied. "They only have four or five guns, I believe, and if we go in a large group and take them by surprise, we can disarm them."

The Griqua men agreed to avoid bloodshed. One evening a large armed group crept up to the rebel colonists' camp. They surrounded Besuitenhout and Vry, catching them by surprise. The two men had been drinking, obviously to excess. They reached for their guns, but saw it was too late.

William who was not armed, acted as spokesman.

"You men have made yourselves highly unpopular in these parts, " he told them. "You threatened the lives of some of our people to whom you deliberately sold a gun with a faulty lock. Not only this, you have stolen cattle and felt nothing about killing innocent Bushmen."

The two men turned abusive, but could do nothing.

William continued,

"We are confiscating your guns and I shall report your presence in these parts to the Landdrost of Tulbagh."

The Landdrost was the chief government official of a district, and acted as its sheriff and judge of sorts. Tulbagh, over 500 kilometres to the south-west, was the nearest significant settlement in the Colony.

William was relieved that things had not gone too badly.

It was only a week or two after this confrontation that William and Kramer discussed Kramer's returning to the Cape. The fugitive colonists were still in the area and were still threatening William and the people with violence, but it was decided that Kramer could still travel with Edwards. He could go via Tulbagh and report recent events to the Landdrost and hand in the confiscated guns.

On the day Kramer and Edwards set off, they heard news that the group of trouble-makers had at last left the Orange

River area. As he travelled south, Kramer had the comfort of knowing that the immediate threat to William and the Griqua community, from Besuitenhout and Vry, had passed.

What he did not know, however, was that the fugitives had left some of their own children behind, having abandoned them when it was discovered that they had come down with the dreaded disease – smallpox.

The killer disease began to spread. Within a month, several Korana had died and the disease had spread to some San villages. It was not long before all the settlements along the Orange were affected.

William tried to persuade all the people to wash their clothing, mostly skins, in an attempt to stop the spread of the smallpox. Few took his suggestions seriously. Some even boasted they would not catch the disease.

---

[26] le Cordeur, Basil A: The Occupations of the Cape, 1795-1854, from An Illustrated History of South Africa, Jonathan Ball Publishers, Johannesburg 1986, p78.
[27] Cape Archives, M304. [28] CWM/LMS/05/02/02/008, Anderson Journal for 1804.
[29] Ibid
[30] Meeting between Governor Janssens and Chief Ngqika, 1803, South African National Library, Cape Town. See also Price, Richard: Making Empire: Colonial Encounters and the Creation of Imperial Rule in Nineteenth Century Africa, Cambridge University Press, Cambridge, 2008.
[31] CWM/LMS/05/02/02/008, Anderson Journal for 1804.

CHAPTER 6:

The Shadow Of Death

William was not finding things easy. Against his advice, several of the men had left their recently-planted gardens and crops of corn and headed north to help Matthias Kok hunt elephant. Kok could make a handsome profit from selling the ivory in the Cape. The men did not seem to care about their families or their cattle.

William found it difficult to deal with the resentment he felt welling up against Kok.

"Missionary? My foot! He should be ashamed of himself," William muttered to himself on more than one occasion. "All our efforts to get these people to settle down and show some sense of responsibility for their families, and then Kok comes along and all they want to do is go off and hunt for him."

On top of this, a group of young Griqua men who had accompanied Kramer south had returned with several horses they had bought in the Colony. They delighted in riding their new acquisitions all over the place in what William thought was a reckless manner, and seemed to enjoy the chaos they created. After several days of wild and noisy horse-racing, an angry William finally told the culprits off.

"Have you fellows gone completely mad? The horses, as well as most of the rest of us, are fed up with all your fooling about!"

William's private and public protestations had little effect. Not surprisingly, those he reprimanded seemed all the more determined to keep at their 'fun'. Not everyone appreciated his efforts, but William meant well and most of the people knew he loved them and had their best interests at heart.

One day in February 1805, a group of men came to see William. They seemed upset and were all talking at once.

"Mijnheer Anderson, you must please come," said one, "Koos has gone blind." Another said, "It happened very suddenly. He is in great pain." Yet another cut in, "Maybe he is dying soon."

When William got to Koos he found he was little more than a skeleton. The poor man could neither eat nor sleep. William sat down next to him and asked,

"Do you have any pain, Koos?"

"No pain, Mijnheer Anderson," came the faint reply.

"Is anything on your mind distressing you?" asked William.

At first Koos gave no answer. William gently persisted and finally, after being asked a few more times, Koos managed a stuttering response.

"Since I went blind, I have been afraid of dying, and I fear I shall be lost forever. I can't eat or sleep," he said.

William, who loved telling people about Christ's forgiveness, gently explained the gospel to Koos. "Koos, even the worst of sinners can be forgiven by Jesus."

William prayed with Koos and over the next few days, visited him several times, often bringing some food to share with him. Within a few days Koos was fully restored. He even got his sight back. The news of his 'miraculous' recovery spread far and wide. Koos became one of the most regular attendants at church, which greatly encouraged William.

William was not one for complaining about his own circumstances, but his poor diet, as well as his primitive living conditions, were affecting his health. His diet consisted mostly of meat and milk, and sometimes even these were in short supply, as was salt which he used as a preservative. At the height of summer, he found himself with no choice at times but to eat 'stinking meat'.[32]

Fortunately, the harvest that year looked as if it would be a good one. It was the first time many of the people had sown crops, and those who had worked hard at their gardens saw a bumper harvest. At three locations – the Kloof, Two Fountains and Klaarwater – they harvested corn. There was real rejoicing.

It was some vindication for William who had been tireless in his efforts to get the people to plant and tend their gardens. However, he gave God the credit. It also meant an improved diet of corn and pumpkins, and a good supply of milk.

The good harvest and his improved diet did not, however, stop William from getting weaker. Despite having no appetite and little strength, he kept busy helping the people, teaching and visiting. Often he had to push himself to work his garden and collect wood and other materials for a new, more permanent house to replace his tiny reed hut.

He also helped organise the digging of water channels and continued making preparations for a move to nearby Klaarwater. Earlier the people had agreed to try to set up a more permanent settlement there. Looking at Klaarwater's excellent spring, William saw potential for agriculture based on irrigation. Klaarwater's spring was perhaps the best in a series of springs that ran some eighty kilometres along the edge of the Asbestos Mountains.

Towards the end of March, a Griqua horseman who had travelled down to the Colony brought a letter from Kramer. It had been five months since William's colleague had left for the

Cape, and this was the first news from him that William had received.

His excitement turned to disappointment, however, as he read the news that Kramer was likely to be further delayed. William began to struggle with self-pity and loneliness. He was now so weak that he could walk only short distances and needed a stick.

The smallpox epidemic was still taking its toll on all the Griqua settlements and William knew he too was seriously ill, though he did not have the typical symptoms of smallpox. He did not know what was afflicting him; it was probably the then unknown disease – malaria.

William found himself praying, "Lord, where are You? I feel as if I'm walking in the darkness with very little light. . . but I will trust You, Lord. I will hold onto Your promises."

He comforted himself with David's words in Psalm 27:13, "I am still confident of this: I will see the goodness of the Lord in the land of the living."

Then things got even worse.[33] For a week or two in April, the smallpox epidemic seemed to reach its height. William began to feel that he and all the people would be swept away by the ravaging disease. Many were ill and there were burials every day. The stench of death seemed to hang in the air.

Despite his own state, William continued to hobble around visiting the sick. He could hardly begin to describe the wretchedness he saw. One of the most distressing cases was that of an attractive young woman. She would scream or groan so pitifully that William could not sleep at night. Her cries carried with an eerie chill around the settlement. She died, – all her beauty distorted in pain and fear. William wept for her, and for many others.

At another home, he could not get near enough a dying woman to hear what she was saying. The stench from her body was just too powerful. The woman's husband said,

"Mijnheer Anderson, just before you came, my wife pleaded with me and the children to accept your message. She said she now knew it was the truth."

By the middle of May, the smallpox epidemic appeared to have abated and most people began to recover.

William, however, only got worse, and many must have thought their teacher would himself soon become one of the victims.[34]

He could no longer walk and was confined to his reed hut. Normally, he kept his hut perfectly clean, but he now found that he did not even have strength to sweep the floor.

His bed was separated from the rest of the room by a curtain; several wooden chests and boxes acted as chairs and a table. William lay on his bed and, looking past the curtain, fixed his eyes on the small prints of English scenery that he had hung from the arching roof of the hut. He had also put up portraits of some of the other missionaries, including James Read and Dr van der Kemp. His eyes could barely see the portraits.

"I doubt I will ever see the shores of England nor the faces of my friends and supporters again – not in this life anyway," he whispered to himself. "I wonder how James is getting on with the doctor among the Xhosa? I doubt I'll see him or Cornelius or my other colleagues again."

He then thought of Johanna and felt a great longing to see her. It comforted him to think of her. He pictured her smile and thought of her steady faith. It somehow reminded him of the hope of a Christian. "Ah! Heaven – should I leave this place it will be but to awake in His presence!" William knew he was dying.

That same day, William was visited by Grick Goejeman, an old woman who was intent on helping him and came often.[35]

"It seems as if I shall die," he told her. As the words passed his parched lips, he felt a great sense of peace that all was well, for God's will was perfect. If he were to die today, he was ready.

His fever raged. At times he was delirious and semi-conscious. The people were helpless. Small groups would gather outside his hut talking in hushed tones.

"When Mijnheer Anderson first came to live among us, we planned to kill him and take his wagon, but now no one wants him to die," said one man almost tearfully.

Piet Pienaar, William's faithful interpreter, attended to him day and night. Whenever Piet came out from the hut, people crowded around him to ask about their teacher's condition.

Aware he was sinking fast, William decided to try to contact three missionaries who had recently travelled up to the Tswana country. Summoning all his strength, he scribbled a note asking them to come and see him. His voice a pitiful whisper, William spoke to Piet Pienaar,

"Piet, ask some of the men to deliver this letter for me. They must not delay. Tell them to ride as fast as they are able."

William did not expect to last long enough to see the men return. He had hardly given the note to Pienaar when he sank into unconsciousness.

The journey to Tswana country usually took about five days, but amazingly, after travelling only two and a half days, the men carrying William's letter met the three missionaries coming in the opposite direction. Within three days of receiving his hardly legible note, they had reached Leeuwenkuil, where William lay delirious.

"The poor man is all but dead," said one of the men, Koster, as he knelt beside William. Koster happened to be a doctor, and set about trying to relieve William's raging fever. It was such a distressing sight that the others in the party hardly dared to look.

Koster remained with William through the night, and was surprised the next day to see him regain consciousness and begin to pull through. The visitors remained for two weeks while William rapidly gained his strength back.

Two of them, including Koster, were married, and their wives busied themselves doing various practical things to help William. He was deeply moved and thanked them again and again. William did not know then, but later he would see a lot more of the third man, a young German called Lambert Jansz.

When the missionaries finally set off, they insisted on giving William two sacks of flour, some tea, coffee, rice, dried fruit, a pair of sheets, two night caps, a pair of long socks, a hat, and some gunpowder and lead. To him, these supplies were priceless.

William was still weak, but the people were clearly over-joyed to see him well on the way to recovery. While thanking the visitors for their timely help, he turned to the large crowd of Griqua and said,

"I also want to thank all of you, and especially my dear brother Piet Pienaar, for your help and loving concern."

Then, turning to Pienaar, he said with tears in his eyes, "Piet, I shall always remember you and dear old Grick Goejeman for all you did for me."

The old lady was there in crowd, smiling from ear to ear.

William and the people stood together waving as their visitors departed. He was full of praise to God for sparing him and for sending relief at just the right moment. He later wrote in his journal,

"However dark it had been for me, the Lord began now to break forth with His light on every side."[36]

Unknown to him, he was soon to receive some other important visitors.

---

[32] CWM/LMS/05/02/02/010, Anderson Journal, December 1804

[33] CWM/LMS/05/02/02/010, Anderson Journal, April 1805

[34] Lovett, Richard: History of the London Missionary Society, 1795-1895, Vol. 1, p 526

[35] CWM/LMS/05/02/02/010, Anderson Journal, May 1805

[36] CWM/LMS/05/02/02/010, Anderson Journal, June 1805

CHAPTER 7:

Visitors

The visitors made quite a sight as they sat huddled in little groups around four or five wood fires. It was 16 June 1805, and the night was extremely cold, one of the coldest William could remember. The visitors had arrived at sunset and immediately set up camp.

There were people of all colours and fashions – blacks from Mozambique in puffy short breeches with turbans on their heads; brown Malays with long black hair twisted up in curls; half-naked San with grey ash smeared all over their bodies; yellow Khoikhoi with skin karosses and caps; Griqua with brown leather waistcoats and breeches, and large white felt hats decorated with black ostrich feathers; white trekboers in fawn suits and leather boots; and Europeans in old, worn-out clothes of various fashions. One was dressed in a shooting jacket, a knitted cap and fur boots, and another was in a uniform, a helmet, and military boots.

Early the following morning, William and several Griqua men went over to greet the visitors who had camped not far from the main Leeuwenkuil settlement. William was particularly pleased to find that some of the visitors spoke English.

Though a motley lot, the expedition party was well equipped. It was led by the Landdrost of Tulbagh, van de Graaff, and Henry Lichtenstein, a German explorer and scientist. Lichtenstein was in his mid-twenties and was a highly erudite though down-to-earth man. He took an immediate liking to William.

"Mr Anderson, it was most distressing what happened last night," he said.

"Do you mean the lion?" asked William.

Lichtenstein nodded.

"Yes! It broke into our camp, dispersed our cattle and carried off our best milking goat. The poor thing was tied to the side of my wagon. We could all hear its pitiful cries, getting fainter and fainter, as the lion dragged it away – but there was nothing we could do about it."

"We also heard the lion and all the commotion it caused," replied William, "but, you are right, there is not much you can do – especially in the dark."

"This morning we traced the path of the 'robber' by following the drops of blood on the snow. It took off up that gully." Lichtenstein pointed to the fortress-like ridge of rocky hills some two hundred metres away from where they stood. It was still bitterly cold but the snow, most unusual for the area, was beginning to melt.

Finding Lichtenstein and the Landdrost warm and friendly, William discussed his work with them and others in the expeditionary party with enthusiasm – blissfully unaware of why they were so interested. Unknown to him, the Dutch authorities in the Cape had instructed the leaders of the expedition to investigate William and assess the validity of the rumours circulating in the Colony that the missionary settlement at the Orange was a hot-bed of subversion against the Cape government.

William, meanwhile, was simply enjoying the stimulation of the interaction; and he particularly valued the chance to get advice from the Landdrost about how he might handle the problems he was facing in the community. He also wanted the government to promise help in ensuring that his people were treated fairly when they went to the Colony to trade. He told the Landdrost of several cases where the Griqua had been exploited.

William took the men to a vantage point from where they could see the whole valley running north from Leeuwenkuil towards the main spring of Klaarwater, some three or four kilometres away. He pointed out the plots of land allocated to different families. Despite the cold weather, the gardens painted a pleasing picture of green in an otherwise bleak landscape. William showed them the irrigation and drainage canals and also the gardens. The visitors were clearly impressed.

At the stone and wood home of a Griqua called Moses Renoseros, the Landdrost asked Moses,

"When did you build this nice house?"

"It was a few months ago, sir," the man replied. "Mijnheer Anderson kept telling us that a house of wood and stone was far better than one made of reeds. He said we would have fewer snakes and scorpions. And . . . ," Moses paused as if to add emphasis, "I find he is right!"

Lichtenstein was fascinated by the stone used to build the house. "This stone is quite remarkable.," he said. "These shiny bands of yellow and brown sparkle beautifully in the sunlight."

The stone had come from nearby ridges of the Asbestos Range, which was composed largely of hard, banded iron-stone. Huge chunks of the 'tiger's eye' rock lay everywhere for the picking.

Neither those in the expeditionary party, nor William and his Griqua friends, were aware of another far more precious stone that lay undiscovered along the banks of the Orange River and in other deposits just a little to their east. Some sixty years later, the 21-carat 'Eureka' diamond and the even larger 83-carat 'Star of Africa' would be discovered. A prospecting rush would create the diamond mining town of Kimberley and catapult it into fame.

Lichtenstein also noticed Moses' flourishing garden with its maize, tobacco, and various vegetables. He whispered to the Landdrost, "I have seldom seen such industry and order in the farms of the Colonists. This is amazing!"

William then took them to the half-finished church building and also told them of his plans to build his own house. The observant Lichtenstein described in detail in his journal what he saw, including William's Korana type reed hut with its English prints and missionary portraits hanging on the roof.[37]

"Mijnheer Anderson, I am most impressed with what you have accomplished with these people," said the Landdrost. "You were asking me how you could maintain good social order. It seems you are doing very well."

But William was not one who liked to make exaggerated claims of success. "Things are not always what they appear on the outside, sir," he said soberly, and continued, "And if anything has been accomplished, it is due solely to the grace of the Covenant God."

The visitors were impressed with William as a man. Their three-day visit was coming to an end. The night before the expeditionary party was to leave, some of its leaders, including the Landdrost and Lichtenstein, had a private discussion about William. Lichtenstein spoke first.

"Hardly a rabble rousing trouble-maker," he said. "Anderson is a quite remarkable man."

The Landdrost agreed, "I too find Mijnheer Anderson most amiable. He has clearly been close to death and is hardly recovered, but I admire his serenity and unassuming self-confidence. He is very pious and totally dedicated to his spiritual mission, yet in no way seems to neglect those activities that would lead to improvement in the livelihood of his people."

Another man, Winterbach, a burgher from the Colony, who was himself a religious man with strong Calvinist beliefs, added,

"Anderson is a saintly man. From when we first met him, I was deeply struck by his personality and manner. Ja, he has a kind of serenity. No sham about his religion."

Lichtenstein nodded. "In addition, he has a good rapport with the people, be they Griqua, Korana or Bushman, and seems to really care for them. Mind you, neither is he taken in by them."

"That's right," added one of the other men. "Anderson himself told us, you remember, that it is often the most lazy and worthless people in the place, some even suspected of attempted murder and robbery, who have the most piety in their mouths."

On the morning of their departure, the Landdrost told William, "Be assured, Mijnheer Anderson, that I will report favourably to the Governor and will recommend to his Excellency that the government actively support you in your work. I will do my best to ensure that colonists, in their barter trade with the Khoikhoi, Griqua and other peoples outside the Colony, hold strictly to fair dealing practices."

William was delighted.

Before the party finally left, the Landdrost urged the people to cooperate with their missionary. He told the large crowd of around 400 that the government was concerned about social order.[38]

William was pleased to get this open support from the Landdrost, but some of the Griqua had their apprehensions. They had enjoyed living far from the restrictions of colonial law, and had resented the degrading prejudice – and sometimes injustice – that most people of colour living within the borders of the Colony had to put up with. The Landdrost represented an authority to which they did not wish to submit.

Nonetheless, the visit had a positive effect upon the people, and William was getting stronger physically by the day. He was full of praise to God.

"Lord, how great and good You are in coming to my aid," he prayed. "My outward situation is as life from the dead."

Still, life was never easy. Trying to build peace between the various groups, and especially with the San, was an on-going struggle.

Over the next few months, there were several incidents involving the San. Cattle were stolen or speared at night, and the Griqua and Korana seemed intent on taking revenge. On one occasion, a group of mostly Korana was mustered to chase the San, but the pursuers ran into an ambush. Despite a hail of San arrows, the guns of the Korana soon dispersed the San, leaving several wounded. At other times, people died in the battles.

All this grieved William. He invited some San to meet him and, through an interpreter, reasoned with them in as warm and friendly a fashion as possible.

"My dear friends," he said, "I have tried to persuade the Griqua and the Korana not to take up arms to settle their disputes with you. Our only weapon should be the weapons of peace and forgiveness. I urge you, from your side, to avoid stealing cattle. You know it leads only to revenge attacks."

The San listened intently, then broke into animated discussion. William had to wait for several minutes before proceeding.

"I want to make you an offer," he finally continued. "I will help you plough some ground and also give you seed."

One of the younger San leaders turned to the others and said, "This is a totally stupid suggestion. We live by hunting. It is a man's pride to be a good hunter. This is our land. The Griqua, the Korana and the Tswana, and more recently the white man, have invaded our ancestral hunting grounds. It is a shame upon us and an insult to our ancestors."

But an older man, whose tufts of short curly hair bore tinges of grey, shook his head. "We need to consider what the white man says," he said. "We all know he is right about stealing and revenge. The revenge goes round in big circles and comes back on our heads worse than before. There can be no end."

A third San warrior screwed up his face and shook his head. "He said we must use weapons of peace. What does he mean? We have our deadly poison arrow heads, they have their spears and guns . . . but what are these weapons of peace?"

Neither William nor his translators, however, heard this discussion.

The tobacco that William offered the San as a sign of friendship was eagerly accepted, and they agreed to consider his proposals further. William longed for a genuine breakthrough.

A few weeks later, the same San leaders came to William and asked to take up his offer. A village of San then moved to Ongeluksfontein, with the blessing of the local Griqua and Korana community.

Meanwhile, William and the leaders of the local Griqua and Korana communities had made what was to prove an important decision. They agreed to move their main settlement from Leeuwenkuil to Klaarwater, about four kilometres north. William had long seen the potential of Klaarwater, with its strong spring and good soil that was suitable for irrigation. Some of the families remained at Leeuwenkuil, but the bulk of the people moved to the new site.

By now, William had been working on his own for over a year. He began to wonder if his colleague Cornelius Kramer would ever return.[39]

37 Lichtenstein, Henry: Travels in Southern Africa in the Years 1803,1804, 1805 and 1806, Becket and Porter, London, 1814. Also various letters of Anderson, CWM/LMS/05/02/02/011.

38 CWM/LMS/05/02/02/010 Anderson Journal for 1805

39 Most details in this chapter come from Andersons letters and journals, CWM/LMS/05/02/02/010 and 011; and from Lichtenstein: Travels in Southern Africa.

CHAPTER 8:

Klaarwater

William was not kept wondering too long. Towards the end of September, Kramer returned at last to the Orange. William was overjoyed to see him. In accordance with a local custom, on the reunion of good friends who had been separated for a long time, the two missionaries each fired a gun in greeting.[40]

Kramer did not return alone for while in the Cape he had found a wife. Mrs Kramer was a young and pretty woman, with dark shoulder-length curly hair which she normally had tied up behind her head. She was from Tulbagh, the seat of the Landdrost, and the third largest town in the Colony after Cape Town and Stellenbosch. Located in a fertile valley in the Cape mountains, Tulbagh was prosperous and the town had many stately Cape Dutch buildings with their typical white gables and shuttered windows. In coming to Klaarwater, Kramer's young wife was coming to a very different world.

The Kramers had brought some letters for William. He could hardly conceal his excitement and joy when he realised one was from Johanna and he read it over and over. He had often thought about her and those thoughts were becoming increasingly romantic. The Kramer's happiness only served to heighten his longing to see Johanna.

"Maybe, with things now a little more settled in my life, I should pluck up the courage to ask her to marry me," he thought.

Another letter was from van de Graaff the Landdrost expressing his personal support for William and the support of the government.[41] A third letter, which confirmed that the Landdrost had indeed reported favourably to the authorities, was from the directors of the SA Society. They informed William that the Military Governor, Janssens, wished to meet him, and suggested that he make a trip to the Cape as soon as he could.[42]

Several months passed, however, before William could leave Klaarwater. Many things kept him tied down. Apart from the building of the church and laying out of new irrigation channels, there was the daily teaching and preaching.

Each morning, the missionaries held a public meeting for prayer, singing and a short sermon. This was done in the 'school house', which was normally filled, and was following by an hour or two of 'school' to teach people to read. By the end of the year, there were about eighty who could read.

The missionaries also took turns to preach three or four evenings a week. At least one of the meetings was interpreted into the Korana language; the rest were all in Dutch. Sundays, meanwhile, were devoted to worship and preaching.

"Cornelius, I believe the regular exposition of Scripture is beginning to bear fruit," said William one Sunday evening as they relaxed before retiring for the day. "The people are becoming more familiar with what it means to be a follower of Christ. And our readings from the works of Francke move not only me, but many of the people."

William was referring to their reading on Sunday afternoons from German Bible scholar August Francke's classic 'The Sufferings of Christ'.

"Did you notice," he continued, "that this afternoon while I was reading of the ill-treatment and abusing of the Lord Jesus before Pilate, that the people seemed very moved?"

"Yes, I did," replied Kramer, "and it was good to see the school house full both times today."

On some Sundays, William and Kramer would take turns to visit some of the near-by settlements to conduct worship services. A trip to the Kloof, about fifty kilometres away from Klaarwater, took about five hours by ox, Khoikhoi-style. If a horse was available, the journey would take less than three hours.

In addition to regular preaching and teaching, William and the Kramers also held many individual conversations with the people about the things of God. One morning in January 1806, after the worship service, William and a young man of about seventeen had a long, congenial chat. William told Kramer about it later.

"Cornelius, I just love such occasions," he said. "The simple way he spoke and the excellent answers he gave to my questions showed the Holy Spirit is truly his teacher, and what I've seen of his life leaves me in no doubt that he is converted."

"What did you say his name was, William?" asked Kramer.

"Andries Waterboer," replied William.[43] Neither he nor Kramer realised that Waterboer was to become one of the most famous Griqua leaders of all time.

The issue of polygamous marriage was one they could not avoid. Many of the Korana men had more than one wife, while some of the Griqua, especially the wealthier ones, had concubines as well.

In one of his sermons, William touched on the subject of polygamy.

"The conversion of a sinner does not consist of leaving this or that sin," he said. "Rather, it involves a total change which begins inwardly and shows itself outwardly. This is a change in a person's whole conduct, both towards God and man. Therefore, until a person is truly converted, it is impossible to see the evil of any particular sin in such a light as to hate and forsake it. We neither can nor would we want to try and force such change."

When a young couple got married, William took the opportunity to teach more about the Biblical view of marriage. He reminded the people of the once common custom among them that allowed a man to separate from his wife easily and, if he wished, to take another wife. The people nodded.

"And you remember all the suffering that would result, don't you?" he said. Again the congregation nodded knowingly.

"So now," continued William, "we must remember that it is not our sinful hearts but the Word of God that must be our guide. What the Bible says about marriage, about the duties of both husband and wife, this is what is important. God wants us to have happy marriages and harmonious homes."

William's teaching on ethics and Christian conduct had an impact on his listeners. Some saw the importance of his preaching of 'inward change which shows itself outwardly' and they experienced the 'change from within effected by divine grace' – as William had expressed it.

Adam Kok, one of the Griqua captains and son of Cornelius Kok, told him later, "Mijnheer Anderson, when you taught us about the Bible and marriage, I thought it was crazy. I remember thinking that it would be impossible to live with only one wife and that I would never give up my concubines." He continued, "The amazing thing is that, while you never forced me, I found myself voluntarily leaving my old life. Through hearing the Word of God, I became convinced of my sin, and found myself wanting to renounce it. Mijnheer, you know little of the terrible lives we lived. We did all we could to keep you in the dark. God changed our hearts, not you."

At times, however, there was a disappointing lack of response and little outward change in people, although the number of true believers was growing slowly.

Apart from spiritual concerns, William & the Kramers were also occupied with practical work. They were kept busy building two new houses, keeping their own gardens, and generally overseeing the multi-faceted activities of the developing settlement.

In the rainy season, they had to contend with hail and floods. One storm saw huge hailstones flatten some of the gardens and the growing corn. Two young men were killed by lightning. On another occasion, during a massive thunder storm, the rain was so heavy it seemed even their homes would be flattened.

Minutes after the rain finally stopped, they heard an ominous rumbling sound in the distance. It got closer and closer, and soon a rising wall of water could be seen coming out of the hills.[44] A surge of seething water engulfed their gardens and fields, then rushed by on both sides of the houses of William and the Kramers.

Everyone desperately tried to divert some of the rushing torrent away from the houses and gardens, with little success. The houses withstood the flooding and the gardens eventually recovered, but the incident motivated them to work harder on digging deeper irrigation channels to the gardens further down the valley.

The ripening grain of harvest time was a temptation to springbok and spring-hare, but more to be feared were locusts. One morning, a huge swarm of locusts appeared on the horizon like a dark cloud. Within an hour, they were flying over Klaarwater, darkening the sky. Capable of turning a green field into a barren wasteland within minutes, the swarm fortunately flew on past Klaarwater.[45]

The people, however, did not escape the masses of little 'tortoise' beetles that did considerable damage to their gardens that year. Another smaller red beetle proved to be the ruin of their cabbages, turnips and radishes, and also seemed to love the leaves of their peas, beans and potatoes.

Despite these setbacks the Klaarwater community was able to enjoy good harvests. By the end of the rainy season, William and the Kramers were able to harvest over 300 large pumpkins and a good supply of potatoes from their gardens alone. These were stacked in their new stone store house.

One morning, while helping to build a water embankment, William was urgently called to help a man with a nasty gunshot wound in his belly.

"What happened?" William asked as he quickly set about cleaning the wound. The man's friends were all talking at once. With gesticulations and in pigeon Dutch, they finally explained, "We were hunting buffalo."

"I should have known as much," said William.

"Koos and I went round to the right and the other two went to the left," one said.

"The buffalo rushed into the tall reeds," another added.

"Yes," said the wounded man, "we knew it was in there, but then we lost sight of those crazy fellows who went left."

"And then?" asked William, almost guessing the answer.

"Next thing, those guys shoot into the reeds. They forget we are opposite them."

William had hardly finished helping the wounded man when a distraught San girl was brought to him.[46] She was bleeding and bruised, having suffered a savage beating from the Griqua woman who had bought her off some Tswana in exchange for a cow several years earlier. William called Mrs Kramer, who took the little girl away to bathe her wounds and apply what salve they had left.

"Will you go home now, my darling?" Mrs Kramer asked gently. The terrified girl shook her head.

Just then, the Griqua woman arrived and angrily demanded that Mrs Kramer return the girl to her. In the middle of her angry outburst, William and Kramer also arrived. On seeing the men, the woman immediately changed her demeanour and tried to appear pleasant and reasonable.

But William, looking her straight in the eye, said sternly,

"You are not fit to have the little girl. Just look at how you've beaten her! No wonder she is terrified of you. Mr and Mrs Kramer will keep her, at least for now. Later, we may reconsider the situation."

Another incident involved the rape of a nine-year old Namaqua girl by a young Griqua man called Jacob Kloete. The girl's father brought her to William and Kramer, who called in two married women to examine the child privately. They confirmed that the little girl did appear to have been raped.

There were no clear laws concerning such a crime, so William called a meeting of all the people. Unanimously, they declared Kloete guilty and said he should be severely beaten. Not knowing what the government in the Cape might expect him to do in such a case, William agreed to hand Kloete over to the leaders of the people, but insisted on being present. He feared they might do worse than beat the culprit.

The public beating was carried out, and the people seemed satisfied that justice had been done. Kloete, however, was angry and abusive.[47]

Almost without realising it, William was being looked to as Klaarwater's judge and protector.

Kramer was regarded by the people as William's assistant, though William himself saw him as an equal. Both men were now acting not only as preachers and teachers, but often also as policemen, doctors, marriage counsellors, agricultural supervisors, and peace keepers. Their work in and around Klaarwater kept them constantly busy.

Yet William knew he needed to make a visit to the Cape.

Almost six months had passed since he was told that Janssens, the Military Governor wanted to meet him.

He also wondered how Johanna was. Would she even recognise him after all this time?

---

[40] CWM/LMS/05/02/02/010, Kramer Journal, July 1805

[41] CWM/LMS/05/02/02/011, Anderson to Hardcastle, 28 August, 1806

[42] CWM/LMS/05/02/02/011, Anderson to LMS, 1 August, 1806

[43] CWM/LMS/05/02/02/011, Anderson Journal, 1806

[44] CWM/LMS/05/02/02/010, Kramer Journal, 19 November, 1805

[45] CWM/LMS/05/02/02/010, Kramer Journal, 21 December, 1805

[46] CWM/LMS/05/02/02/010, Anderson Journal, 1805

[47] CWM/LMS/05/02/02/011, Anderson Journal, 28 March, 1806

CHAPTER 9:

Caught In The Flood

"What do you make of it, Cornelius?" William asked as he handed the letter back to Kramer, surprise written all over his face. "Our friends at the Zak must have heard an accurate report – 'Cape once again in the hands of the British' – but that is all. No more detail than that."

"William, who knows? At least it is not the French who have taken over!" Kramer paused, then continued thoughtfully, "If the Dutch are out, you may have missed your appointment with Governor Janssens."

"I feel bad about that. A missed opportunity."

"You couldn't have gone any earlier, William," Kramer said reassuringly. "However, if there is a new government in power in the Cape, there might be even more reason to visit."

Both Kramer and William knew that even events in the far-off Cape could affect the lives of those living at the Orange River.

"You're right," agreed William. "Perhaps I should not delay my visit any longer."

It was the last day of March, 1806. Like the ox wagon, news had travelled slowly, and political events had not waited for William. Over the past few months, he had found himself torn between visiting the Cape and staying in Klaarwater.

The situation was anything but settled. There had been serious clashes between groups of Tswana and the San. In one battle alone, eighteen San had been killed, their simple shelters razed to the ground, and men, women and children mutilated. The Tswana accused the people of Klaarwater – by then numbering nearly 800[48] – of instigating the trouble by encouraging the San to steal their cattle.

It was not the first, nor the last time, that untrue rumours were being spread. The Tswana had not attacked Klaarwater, but were threatening to do so.

William the peacemaker grieved over the on-going conflict. He pleaded with his people and with both Tswana and San to use 'weapons of peace'. Love and acceptance could flow between peoples, if only they would receive God's redeeming love into their lives. It was William's heart cry for Africa.

Finally, towards the end of April, William was ready to leave.

On the day of his departure, a large crowd of well-wishers turned up to see their teacher and pastor leave. Many openly shed tears. William assured them he would return as soon as possible. After singing and praying with the Kramers and the people, he jumped up onto the wagon beside Old Solomon, one of his faithful Griqua friends.

Then, looking back and waving once more, he felt a lump in his throat. The Kramers were standing together, Mrs Kramer holding her tiny son who had been born just one month earlier. William had seen how married life had brought such joy to Kramer and even increased his effectiveness in his missionary work.

William was excited at the prospect of seeing the Schonken family – especially Johanna – again. He had a secret known only to himself. He was going to ask Johanna to marry him and if she agreed he would bring her back to Klaarwater as his wife.

"Life would not be easy for her," he thought, "but at least she would have a good companion in Mrs Kramer."

Klaarwater was soon out of sight. William thought about the many difficulties the Kramers were likely to face in his absence. Little did he know, he was soon to face grave danger himself.

William and his party of Griqua friends met up with Mr and Mrs Edwards with whom they were to travel to the Cape.

Edwards was the Englishman who had found it so difficult to work with Kicherer at the Zak River. He had since married and joined Matthias Kok and his family in their missionary and trading activities in Tswana territory. Now he and his young wife were travelling to the Cape to escape some of the inter-tribal and inter-clan conflict that was plaguing the Tswana. Their journey had been delayed by the rain and flooding, which made it difficult to cross the Orange River.

For several days, the men searched for possible crossing points along the river. But everywhere water levels were too high for the wagons to cross safely. They would just have to be patient.

The time was not wasted for William, however, as he made contact with local groups of San and Korana. On one occasion, he was left almost alone, as the majority of the travelling party had decided to go hunting. Hunting was not something William enjoyed.

All of a sudden, a group of San men, women and children appeared. They ended up spending most of the day together. William was nowhere near fluent in their strange tongue-clicking language,[49] but with a mixture of Dutch, Korana and some 'Bushman', together with liberal use of sign language, he managed to communicate with the San.

As the sun dipped below the horizon with its multi-coloured splendour, the visitors slipped away quietly. Not long after, the hunting party returned, full of excitement about their exploits.

William, however, was not at all envious. He had had a far more interesting day with his San friends.

Two weeks had passed, and still the level of the water had not dropped enough for a safe crossing. One of the Griqua men tried to ride his horse through at various places, but struggled against the force of the water. A few days later, the level of the water seemed to have reduced further, and some of the men, including William, tried wading through. Again, they were without success.

"Monday should be OK," said Peter Cariend, one of the men. "If the water recedes just a little more, I am sure we will be able to make it." Others nodded in agreement.

It was Saturday, and there was heavy rain that night. William found it almost impossible to sleep, for he had been bedded down on the ground under one of the wagons. Early in the morning, a Griqua man rode in from Kloof, which was further upstream, and informed them that the water level was rising.

"Before too long the rising waters will reach you, and then you will be delayed for many more days," he said, gesticulating excitedly. "If you delay your crossing until tomorrow, it may be too late!"

One of the men, who had just been examining the spot chosen for their planned crossing, said, "It seems safe to cross. The level is not too high."

William preferred not to travel on a Sunday if he could help it. He and Edwards discussed the situation while the other men stood by, listening.

"It appears we should make a move as soon as possible and trust ourselves into the hands of our Covenant God," said William.

"I too would prefer to wait till tomorrow, but I fear that may not be wise," said Edwards. Their Griqua friends agreed, and the party immediately prepared to cross the Orange.

At the point chosen for the crossing, the Orange River was split into two channels, with a small island in the middle. The sheep and cattle, which were needed for meat, milk and occasionally for bartering, were swum across to the island safely, and the two wagons also made it without any trouble. Everyone was relieved.

However, there was still the second channel. The men swam some of the animals through and Edwards' sturdy old wagon loaded with their possessions, also got through without difficulty.

William's wagon was next. Together with Edwards, his wife and little daughter, William held on tightly as the team of eight oxen was urged forward into the water by one of the Griqua herdsmen.

Just at that moment, the first pair of oxen suddenly veered round, throwing the rest of the team into confusion. Within seconds, some of the oxen lost their footing, and they and the wagon were swept downstream.

"It's impossible to save the wagon!" shouted John Schryver, one of the men. "Mijnheer Anderson, throw off your heavy clothes and boots! We're finished! Jump!"

William caught Edwards' eye. They both knew that if they were swept into the deep hippo pools, there would be little hope. Almost on impulse, Edwards jumped into the water and swam back to the island, which was still close by. Very soon, the wagon was in the middle of the channel and drifting ever closer to where the two channels met. At that point, the water was very deep.

Again, one of the men shouted to William, "Mijnheer, jump in! Swim!"

By now, the men were all in the water and trying to steady the floating wagon. The less weight in the wagon, the more chance they had to steady it. William realised this, but he had another dilemma. How could he leave Mrs Edwards and the child?

"The lighter the wagon, the better. I must get out," he told Mrs Edwards, trying to keep calm. "It will be easier for the men. Just hold on tightly."

Mrs Edwards hardly heard him. She and her little girl were terrified. As he jumped into the water, William heard Mrs Edwards crying out, "Lord Jesus! Lord Jesus, save us!"

Two of the men came to William's assistance as he floundered in the swirling water, but he was able to swim. As he struggled towards the south bank of the river, he began to feel so weak that he started to wonder if he would make it. For a few moments, fear gripped his mind. Just as he gave up hope, however, a teenage Korana lad grabbed his arm and helped him get to the bank. Still gasping for breath, he turned round to see what had happened to the wagon and its precious human cargo, fearing the worst.

Just before the wagon reached the hippo pools, the oxen managed to regain their footing. Four of the men, all good swimmers, managed to steady the floating wagon, with Mrs Edwards and her daughter still desperately clinging on inside. Finally, with the oxen straining for shore, the men helped pull the wagon to safety on the southern side of the river.

An overjoyed Edwards swam over from the island with the last two men. William too was very relieved.[50]

There was much rejoicing. The travellers had their Sunday worship service and gave praise to God for their deliverance. Some items had been lost and everything was soaked except, fortunately, their carefully wrapped powder for the guns and a parcel containing letters and journals.

The next day, they swam the remaining animals over from the island and being a sunny day they lay everything out to dry. On the Wednesday they continued south towards the Cape, leaving the Orange River further and further behind them. The next nine days were by no means uneventful, but in the evening of 19 May, they arrived safely at the Zak River.[51]

There, William was delighted to find a letter from his dear friend Joseph Hardcastle, the LMS Treasurer in London. The letter was dated 9 April, 1805; it had taken over a year to reach him. In his letter, Hardcastle told William that he and all the directors and supporters of the LMS were thrilled about the news they had received of William's work among the Korana. He also wrote about the LMS's growing work in India and Ceylon, and added, "China has become an object of our serious attention."

The first recruit for the mission to China was preparing himself in London, and was described by Hardcastle as "a pious and able young man . . . who has made considerable progress in acquiring some rudiments of the language".[52] That young man was Robert Morrison, who was later to become the first Protestant missionary to China.[53]

William and the Edwards left the Zak and soon after, met Lambert Jansz, one of the three missionaries who had come to William's aid when he was dying at Leeuwenkuil. Jansz, who was on his way north, gave them more news of events at the Cape.

With war breaking out again between Britain and France, the British had decided that the Cape was of strategic value in their imperial and commercial rivalry with Napoleon. Troops were sent to the Cape in January under the command of General Sir David Baird, landing at Blaauwberg beach, near Cape Town, where they engaged in a short but fierce battle with Dutch troops. The British lost about 200 men while the Batavians lost about 350 men. The remaining Dutch soldiers surrendered to the British.

"What happened to Janssens?" asked William. He had been looking forward to meeting the now deposed Dutch Military Governor.

"He and his remaining troops retreated to the Hottentots Holland Mountains and finally, eight days later, surrendered to the British," replied Jansz. "This all happened five months ago, of course, and already the British are firmly in control."

William did not yet know it, but in just a few short weeks he was to be ushered in to see the new Acting British Governor.

Something else William did not know at the time was that a certain Henry Martyn had been travelling with the British forces when they defeated the Batavians. Serving as chaplain to the British forces, tending dying soldiers, and seeing the horrors of war convinced Martyn that Britain should seek to convert, not colonize, the world. He wrote in his diary, "I prayed that. . . England whilst she sent the thunder of her arms to distant regions of the globe, might not remain proud and ungodly at home; but might show herself great indeed, by sending forth the ministers of her church to diffuse the gospel of peace."[54] William would have been in full agreement with Martyn's sentiments. Martyn was soon to begin his brief but famous missionary career amongst Muslims in India and Iran.

After meeting Jansz, William and his party hurried on their way. By this time the Cape was well into winter. It was cold and wet as they made their way through the Roggeveld Mountains, where they travelled through some heavy snowfalls. Waking up one morning after having spent the night wrapped up in blankets under the wagon, William felt icicles in his hair.

After a brief six-day stop-over in picturesque Tulbagh, where he visited several friends including the family of Mrs Kramer, William took leave of the Edwards and most of his Griqua companions, and headed eagerly for Cape Town.

On 7 July 1806, William finally reached Cape Town. The thought of meeting his many friends excited him, but nothing excited him more than knocking on the door of the Schonken home. When he saw Johanna, his heart seemed to be beating so fast he could hardly speak.

"You haven't changed," he said with a slight stutter. Somehow she looked even more beautiful than before. Tears of joy glistened in her dark brown eyes.

"William, we are so relieved to see you alive!" She looked at him and continued hesitantly, "But you look much thinner."

"We never forgot to pray for you," said Mrs Schonken.

"No, not even for a single day," added Johanna.

When William and Johanna found themselves alone, he plucked up courage to take her hand. "Johanna, I love you," he whispered.

She nodded. "I love you too, William. With all of my heart." Both of them knew they were meant for each other.

---

[48] Ibid

[49] J. D. Lewis-Williams: The San: Life, Belief and Art in An Illustrated History of South Africa, Jonathan Ball Publishers, Johannesburg, 1986, pages 31-33.

[50] CWM/LMS/05/02/02/011, Anderson Journal, April, 1806

[51] Ibid

[52] CWM/LMS/05/02/02/011, letter from Hardcastle & Burder in London, 14 July 1806

[53] Horne, Silvester: The Story of the London Missionary Society, London 1908, p 107ff.

[54] McManners, John: Oxford Illustrated History of Christianity. Oxford University Press, 1990, 457

CHAPTER 10:

Love Blossoms

The question of their daughter's marriage was discussed by the Schonkens on several occasions, the last of which took place just a few days before Bartholomew Schonken's unexpected death.

"Dear, I can't help wondering if Johanna will ever marry," he told his wife. "She is already close to thirty and has shown little interest in any of the fine men we considered suitable. She could have been married several times by now!"

"She has not yet found the right man, Bartholomew," interjected Mrs Schonken.

"Naturally it would be most fitting for her to marry a Dutchman," continued Mr Schonken. "Certainly this would be preferable to her finding an Englishman."

Mr Schonken paused and then, as if reluctantly yielding to some unspoken argument, added, "Well, maybe that is prejudice . . . After all there are some very fine Englishmen. Take William Anderson, for example. I took a liking to him almost from the moment I met him the day he and his LMS colleagues arrived at the Cape. He is a good man. He clearly respects our language and culture and, were it not for the undoubted hardships she would have to face, I would have no objection to Johanna marrying him. Mind you, he is not young anymore either."

Mrs Schonken nodded. "I think he is almost thirty-six, Bartholomew, but that still sounds young to me. Mr Anderson is a fine man, but I doubt he has much interest in marriage."

Apart from the Kramers and Johanna's sister, Maria, few had any idea that William and Johanna had been interested in each other. But now that William had openly proposed marriage, most thought it must have been a whirlwind romance.

Johanna's mother, who only a few months earlier had faced the sadness of her husband's passing, was overjoyed. She immediately gave her blessing, knowing that her husband too would have given his approval. While it would not be easy for Johanna to join William in his lonely and dangerous work, she knew that her daughter, a devout Christian, would make a gifted and faithful wife for William.

The next six weeks were frantically busy for William and Johanna. There were many friends to see and seemingly endless preparations to be made, not just for the wedding day, but for the future. They treasured the times they could be alone to talk. William was open about the privations Johanna might expect.

"Life is hard north of the mountains, and even harder north of the Orange. It is a violent and cruel world," he said as they sat together on the back stoep of the Schonken home. It was an unusually pleasant sunny day after several days of cold winter drizzle.

"Those who know me best, my sweetheart, would surely have expected me to have given up by now."

William looked tenderly into Johanna's eyes, and continued seriously, "I love the people and I love the country, but there have been times when I felt I would rather be anywhere but at the Orange. Yet strange as it may seem, Johanna, despite the difficulties, I regard north of the Orange, living with the Griqua, the Korana, the Bushmen and the Tswana, to be the happiest place in the world. I am in the very place where my Lord wants me."

"William, darling," Johanna said, taking both his hands and squeezing them, "I have prayed daily for you and the people at the Orange and more and more I feel it is also the very place He has chosen for me to be. The people of your heart are the people of my heart also."

William sneaked a quick, but long to be remembered, kiss. Though soon to be married, it was not the-done-thing to be seen kissing in public.

After a long silence he continued,

"You know, Johanna, it may seem a strange thing, but I preach the gospel with more delight and liberty in Dutch than I ever did in my own native tongue."

Johanna smiled. She remembered how William had once struggled with his Dutch. "I think I have made a little progress with my English too, you know," she said with a chuckle.

Another sunny day greeted the occasion of their wedding on 17 August 1806. It was a festive occasion and the Dutch Church was filled with friends and well-wishers from all social and racial backgrounds. There were even a few of William's Griqua friends sitting in the congregation, beaming from ear to ear.

Proposing marriage had not been the only matter on William's mind when he arrived in Cape Town early in July. There was also the urgent need to meet with the new British authorities. On his way to Cape Town, William had been warmly received by the Landdrost in Tulbagh.

"Mijnheer Anderson, I can assure you that, had the Cape remained in the hands of the Dutch, you would have found the authorities highly favourable towards you. You would have been free to continue your work with their full approval. What the attitude of the new government will be, I cannot say."

Arriving in Cape Town, William noticed that his clothes were distinctly shabby compared with the fashion-conscious citizens of the 'big city'. He counted his money carefully and visited a tailor. When his new suit was ready, he sought an interview with the Acting Governor General, Sir David Baird. Permission was given and on the appointed day, William was escorted past the guards and into the Castle to meet General Baird.[55]

"Good day, Mr Anderson," the General said, shaking William's hand warmly. "I have heard quite a lot about you and your institution north of the Orange River. It gives me great pleasure to be able to meet you and learn from you first-hand about the situation as you see it."

William was impressed by the General's keen interest in his work; it seemed he was not averse to spiritual things either. They chatted in a relaxed manner for at least an hour, during which William told General Baird about life in the interior. He also took the opportunity to plead for the new government to show a favourable attitude towards missionary work.

"Mr Anderson, I can assure you that I will give you all possible assistance and protection," General Baird said. "I am not happy, however, about the fact that so many of your people are armed with guns. This could in future prove to be a de-stabilising factor on the northern borders of the Colony."

"Honourable sir," replied William, "the Griqua, and to some extent the Korana also, rely upon their arms for survival, mainly because they have to hunt to supplement their food supplies. They are not skilled, as the Bushmen, with the bow and arrow, nor like the Tswana, with the spear. In addition, they need arms for protection against wild animals. I myself have had some close encounters with lions and other dangerous beasts."

William did admit, however, that his people were only too ready to use their arms against the San, especially when the latter stole cattle and sheep. The killing of the San, however, appeared to be more of concern to him than it was to the British officials.

"My concern, Mr Anderson, is not with the Bushmen but rather with the threat posed to the Colony by armed peoples on our borders," the General observed.

Still, much to William's relief, the issue of guns was the only point of contention in an otherwise very friendly encounter with Governor Baird.

Later, after receiving a petition signed by some of the directors of the SA Society, General Baird gave permission for William to be issued with fifty pounds of gunpowder and one hundred pounds of lead when he returned to the Orange.[56] The authorities tried to keep a strict control on the supply of gunpowder.

William, meanwhile, was being careful with his money. He needed to buy a new wagon, but was concerned that it was a big expense for the LMS. Not wishing to be a burden to supporters in England, he seldom requested financial assistance from the LMS, and often went without some of the things others regarded as necessities.

Being also reserved, cautious and often self-effacing, he avoided writing long and glowing reports of his work.

"Some people exaggerate, perhaps not deliberately, but to me exaggeration is dishonesty," he confided in Johanna. "I fear our supporters in Europe would feel let down should our claims of success later prove to be premature."

William's reluctance to write about his experiences and work meant that few in Europe got to know of his accomplishments. Unlike some other more 'famous' missionaries he never returned to England to report on his work. While in Cape Town, however, both before and after his marriage to Johanna, he did write several long letters and reports to the directors in London.

"I would not exchange my Mission for any one in Africa,"[57] he wrote. "We have been enabled to endure severe storms, but our blessed Redeemer was with us in the same and has granted us now a pleasant calm. Oh, that He may keep us humble, faithful and diligent."

In one letter, dated 27 August 1806, he asked if the LMS could send "cloth, linen, stocking and implements of husbandry", as well as other tools from England. Such things were very expensive in the Cape. He also asked for two diamonds to cut glass.[58] Had William known about those as yet undiscovered diamond deposits not far from Klaarwater, he might not have bothered to ask for the diamonds.

William felt ten years younger. He was full of praise to God for enabling him to get so much accomplished, but what was even more wonderful to him was the fact that he now had Johanna as his wife and companion. Their first few weeks of married life had been very happy, although there was no time for a relaxed and romantic honeymoon: It was a whirl of activity.

It was not easy for Johanna to say good-bye to her many friends and relatives. It was particularly hard to leave her mother, whom she had always been very close to. Early on 10 September, William and Johanna waved to a crowd of friends and well-wishers as they climbed up onto the horse-drawn carriage that would take them to Tulbagh. From there some of the people from Klaarwater would accompany them back to the Orange River. Their new ox wagon, loaded with supplies, had gone on ahead of them to Tulbagh a few days earlier.

The driver of the carriage cracked his whip, a signal the horses knew meant it was time to move. With William and Johanna were some of Johanna's closest friends who had decided to accompany her as far as Tulbagh. The sun's rays were just beginning to spill over the mountain peaks to the east. As they set off, William and Johanna had little idea of the dangers that awaited them on their 'honeymoon' journey.

---

[55] CWM/LMS/05/02/02/011, Anderson to Hardcastle, from Cape Town, 28 August, 1806

[56] Ibid

[57] Ibid

[58] Ibid

CHAPTER II:

Tragedy Averted

*T*ulbagh was beautiful after the winter rains, and spring was evident everywhere. It's neat buildings, so typical of the Cape Dutch style with their white-washed walls, colourful wooden shutters, arching gables and thatched roofs, stood in civilised contrast to the rugged beauty of the towering mountains surrounding the town. Tall oak trees drew their nourishment from the fertile, well-watered soil of the Klein Berg River valley.

Johanna said tearful good-byes to her Cape Town friends, and a few days later, she and William bade farewell again to friends in Tulbagh.

Their departure was quite a sight. The procession out of town included a white missionary with his young bride, an excited group of Griqua, many proudly riding on horses, a new wagon, sheep, goats and oxen. The party headed eastwards towards a gap in the mountains where the rushing waters of the Hex River forced their way southwards to join the Breede River.

The journey through the Cape mountains and up the Hex River valley was no easy venture. The young oxen, unused to being in yoke and having to struggle through boulder-strewn torrents, made slow and reluctant progress as they pulled the heavily loaded wagon. After four days of weary travel, they arrived at the foot of the magnificent Hex River mountains.

"Vielen dank, Mijnheer Jordaan," William called as he waved good-bye to the friendly trekboer who had offered his own oxen to help pull them over the steepest parts. It had not been free labour, for William was six Rixdollars poorer, but he was none the less grateful. They had made it over the mountains.

For ten days they made steady progress through the flat and increasingly dry country-side, known as the Karoo.

"I was told that the word Karoo comes from a Khoikhoi dialect and means 'dry land'," William explained to Johanna. "It really is dry north of the Hex River mountains."

"There is so little for our cattle and sheep to eat," Johanna said, looking around at the sparse vegetation. There was little more than low shrubs and clumps of grass.

"It is actually even drier once we get through the Roggeveld mountains," said William.

The Roggeveld mountains were even more of an obstacle than the Hex River mountains. The tired oxen had no strength left for any attempt at pulling the wagon up the steep slopes.

"What do you think we should do?" William asked the men. He valued their opinions and worked closely with them.

"Some of us can go off early in the morning to look for help," one suggested.

It was an isolated area, but they found a farmer, Jaspar Cloete, and he agreed to lend them his oxen for a fee of ten Rixdollars. Cloete and a friend, Botha, brought a team of twelve fresh animals, which they hitched up in pairs. They made good progress up the mountain.

Johanna rode a horse behind the wagon, turning in the saddle frequently to take in the beautiful views.

Most of the Griqua men were up ahead, driving the sheep and cattle. A few were helping to urge on the oxen pulling the wagon. Everything seemed to be going well until they reached about halfway up the mountain.

Here, Botha thought it would be better if they re-arranged two of the oxen.

"Them two is not pulling good together," he said in his broken English.

William could see that one of the two oxen was a little wild and was jerking its head impatiently. Without word or warning, Botha unyoked the two oxen, which were in the second row from the wagon.

Pandemonium broke loose immediately. As the first five pairs of oxen were suddenly relieved of their load, the full weight of the heavily-laden wagon was left resting entirely on the necks of the two oxen nearest the wagon. It was far too heavy for them and they were dragged backwards. The wagon slid off the narrow track and it seemed as if nothing would prevent it from tumbling over the edge of the cliff – taking with it Johanna, who was right behind.

"Johanna!" William screamed, "Look out! The wagon! Jump for it!" He rushed towards her, but it seemed hopeless. She had no way to get out of the path of the sliding wagon. Her horse, sensing the impending danger, reared up on its hind legs and threatened to send Johanna flying. She desperately clung on to the saddle.

In those moments of horror, all the men could do was watch helplessly. Adam Balie, however, one of the Griqua men from Klaarwater threw himself towards the last two oxen, cracking his whip. The sudden sting of the whip made the animals pull forward, and as they did so Balie threw a chain around one wheel of the wagon. Dropping the whip he then grabbed a few large stones and quickly wedged them behind the wheels. Disaster was averted by his swift and skilful intervention.

William reached Johanna, helped her down off the horse, and hugged her tightly. They were both shaking with fright.

Cloete glared at his friend Botha but said nothing. They were too relieved to start recriminations, and were not yet over the mountain.

Order was restored among the oxen, and after further pulling and whipping, shouting and shoving, they finally reached the top in the late afternoon. It had taken them over four hours to haul the wagon up the mountain. Cloete apologised profusely as he took leave of the party. He was not a very religious man, but admitted God had delivered them from disaster.

That night, as they prayed together, William and Johanna, still a little shaken from the ordeal, thanked God for preserving them.[59]

The next morning, William encouraged the party and prayed for courage and protection as they continued towards their destination. They still faced the threat of sudden attacks by the San, who were sometimes hostile and were known to steal cattle and sheep, and murder travellers.

"When the Bushmen appear with their wives and children," William explained to Johanna, "we have little reason to fear. It is when we observe fresh footprints, but see no one, that we need to be more on our guard. We can't blame them for feeling threatened; after all, we are passing through their hunting lands. How are they to know we want only to be their friends?"

Six weeks after leaving Cape Town, William and Johanna arrived at the Zak River, only to find Kicherer's 'mission station' deserted.[60] The first attempt to establish a mission to the San had clearly floundered. William could not help feeling a great sense of disappointment. He wondered how he would find things at Klaarwater.

"Johanna, remember those rumours that we heard from that Korana just after we crossed the Roggeveld?"

"Yes – that the Kramers had left and Klaarwater was abandoned," replied Johanna.

"I am sure they are only empty rumours sent to try us. However, seeing these ruins of a work started in faith makes me wonder. What makes a work successful? How does one measure success? What leads a man to give up when he once had such hope?"

Johanna could see that William was most concerned about things in Klaarwater.

Later, William would discover why Kicherer had given up at the Zak. The cultural differences between the Khoikhoi and the San were so great that Kitcherer saw little hope of establishing a permanent work among them. On top of this, the physical hardships were more than what most could stand; life was not easy in these dangerous and uncertain arid lands.

After some time, Kicherer had accepted an invitation to become a minister of the Dutch church in Graaff-Reinet, a settlement established on the upper Sundays River just south of the Sneeuwberg mountains further east. Graaff-Reinet, which commanded three routes over the mountains, including one to the Orange River, had become the most important settlement on the eastern frontier of the Colony.

The Andersons were now well beyond the northern borders of the Colony. They had left the Zak and continued northwards, where the land became increasingly parched and barren.[61]

"Mijnheer Anderson, we hardly have enough water for our own drinking, let alone for the animals," said Ian Hendrick, one of William's most trusted Griqua friends. "I fear the animals will begin to die. The sheep are so thirsty they begin to wander and it is almost impossible to keep them together."

William tried to reassure Johanna but like the men found it hard not to be a little anxious. There was indeed very little drinking water left in the canvas water bottle tied to the side of the wagon. Their other containers were already empty.

Relief came just in time.

"Water, Mijnheer Anderson! Water!" The men shouted excitedly. "There is enough for ourselves and also plenty for the sheep." The little fountain, called Mudderfontein, had enough water to satisfy all but the most thirsty oxen.

Finally, almost two months after leaving Cape Town, they reached the Orange River. The plentiful water and the tree-lined valley was such a welcome sight that it proved too much for Johanna. As she and William sat together on the river bank, drinking in the colours of the glorious sunset, she could not hold back her tears of joy and relief. They were now just a few day's journey from Klaarwater, which was on the other side of the Orange River.

This time the level of water was much lower than the last time William had made the crossing. They had little difficulty getting the wagon and animals through.

It took them two days to swim all the animals across, during which they lost only three sheep. In addition to their oxen, they had brought two hundred and thirty one sheep, five goats, and two horses all the way from Cape Town.[62]

As they were setting up camp for the night after having completed the crossing, a group of San approached. Johanna swallowed hard and looked at William in apprehension. But the San were no strangers to him. They were most friendly, and they also brought news that made William literally jump for joy: Everything was fine at Klaarwater.

A week after crossing the Orange, they finally approached the settlement about which Johanna had heard so much. They received a chaotic but happy welcome, as a crowd of Klaarwater residents swarmed excitedly around, all wanting to get a closer look at William's new bride.

The Kramers and their little boy were overjoyed to see William and Johanna. Johanna and Mrs Kramer took an immediate liking to each other; and the two women being descended from early Dutch families in the Cape had a lot in common.

Also in the welcoming party was Lambert Jansz, whom William had met on his way down to the Cape. Jansz was one of the three missionaries who had found William close to death over a year earlier.

"What a pleasant surprise to see you, Lambert my brother!" William called out above the hullabaloo.

"I've finally come to retrieve my belongings," Jansz shouted back. Several months earlier, after abandoning his attempt to settle among the Tswana people further north, he had left most of his possessions stored in boxes in Klaarwater.

As the people pressed around them William proudly introduced Johanna to one after another of his Griqua and Korana friends. Young Andries Waterboer gave William a big wink of approval.

Klaarwater was soon to feel like home to Johanna.

---

[59] CWM/LMS/05/02/02/012, Anderson to LMS, 1 September, 1807
[60] Ibid
[61] Ibid
[62] Ibid

CHAPTER 12:

Peace-Makers

*T*he air was cool in the late afternoon, and William, Kramer and Jansz were out walking and catching up on each other's news.[63] They were engrossed in conversation and were some distance away from the settlement when they heard someone running in their direction, urgently calling for them. The messenger was out-of-breath, and could say little more than that they should return home immediately.

Kramer looked at William.

"I hope our wives and the child are safe," he said anxiously.

"Me too," replied William, as the three of them took to their heels.

They were relieved to see Johanna and Mrs Kramer waiting for them. With them were two visiting Korana Khoikhoi who were still on their horses. They repeated their message in a mixture of broken Dutch and Korana. William understood immediately.

"The missionary trader Kok has been murdered by the Tswana," he told the others. "Mrs Kok is distraught and she too fears for her life."

The Koks had been living among the Tswana to the north and had been engaged in bartering for ivory. Matthias Kok had not exactly endeared himself to the locals. He had a strong personality and had struck many a hard bargain. As a result, he and the Tswana had little in common.

"What tragic news," said William, shaking his head. "I always feared Brother Kok would get himself and his family into trouble. He was not wise in his dealings with the Tswana, nor did he seem seriously committed to missionary endeavour."

Nevertheless, the news of Kok's murder came as a shock. William and the others immediately organised a party of men to go and help the distressed Mrs Kok and escort her to Klaarwater, where the Kramers and Andersons would later give her much comfort and help.

For Johanna, the sad saga underlined the fact that she was a long, long way from the comfort and safety of Cape Town. In marrying William, she had not chosen an easy life. She was joining him in the war zone of conflicting cultures.

Something else was beginning to concern Johanna. About six months earlier, some of the men had shot a lioness in the fields, then discovered that she had three tiny cubs. They must have been only about two weeks old. The men had brought the orphaned cubs to William, who had decided to feed and care for them.

"Maybe we can have them sent down to Cape Town when they are a little bigger," he suggested to a somewhat sceptical Johanna. "We might be able to tame them and there would be great interest in the animals."

Over the months, however, the three cubs were becoming noticeably larger and were eating more and more. Even William began to have doubts about the wisdom of keeping them. Gone was the cuddly sweetness of the first few months. They were becoming quite dangerous.

One of the Griqua captains told William when they discussed the problem, "Little lions become big lions and big lions kill. Mijnheer Anderson, those young lions must be shot."

William knew that he was right, no matter how attached he had become to his pets.

Another thing that grieved William was the ever-fragile relations between the Griqua and the San. William had told Johanna about previous incidents, and she began to share his concern. Now, within a month of their arriving in Klaarwater, they were to see the old pattern of spiralling violence.

A report that some San had stolen a few cattle and sheep sparked an immediate and angry response among the Griqua. Many rushed to pick up their weapons, and a large group of men were soon assembled, ready to set off in hot pursuit. William desperately tried to reason with them.

"My friends," he pleaded, "we have warned you not to neglect your animals. When you leave them unattended for days on end, it can only be a temptation to the Bushmen. If now, by taking revenge, you shed blood, that blood will be on your own heads."

But the men were in no mood to listen.

The missionaries, joined by some of the Klaarwater Christians, could only pray.

The men returned four days later. Blood had indeed been shed.

The pursuing party had found some of the stolen animals, and as they approached an area of thick bushes, they were suddenly met with a volley of arrows. Having no idea of how many San were hidden in the thick foliage, the enraged Griqua simply fired a ferocious barrage with their guns. After the thunderous roar of the guns faded away and the smoke dissipated, two men and a woman lay dead in pools of blood. The rest of the San had fled.

Setting off in hot pursuit, the armed posse came upon a frightened group of San women and children. They left the women unmolested but seized seven of the children. It was an old custom for victors to kidnap children to use as slaves.[64]

Only later was William able to convince the people that they should not take children unless both parents were dead and the children were unable to survive on their own.

Savage fighting also broke out frequently between Korana Khoikhoi and various groups of Tswana, largely as a result of cattle rustling.

Like many of the other black tribes, the Tswana were not a homogenous group, but consisted of various clans. A powerful leader might be able to weld several clans into a strong federation, but could do little to eliminate inter-clan rivalry and feuding. Groups of Xhosa from east and south of the distant Sneeuberg Mountains were also marauding in areas close to Tswana-dominated territory, which further unsettled the Tswana. Life was cheap, and armed conflict seemed the only way to settle any dispute.

Rumblings of trouble between the Griqua Korana community in Klaarwater and the Tswana also began to threaten the peace. One day, in the early hours, William was woken by two Griqua banging urgently on the door.

"Mijnheer Anderson, the Tswana have chased the people from Tweefontein and they say they will attack Klaarwater! They are armed and breathe murder! What can we do?"

William quickly dressed and rang the bell to call the people. It was still dark but soon, everyone had gathered and crowded around a hurriedly-lit bonfire. They listened in trepidation as some of the men described how the Tswana would attack a place just before dawn, approaching in total silence then setting the houses on fire.

"They stand at the door of each burning hut and mercilessly stab those inside as they come out trying to escape the flames," said one man.

Though the Griqua had guns, and the Tswana did not, William urged that every attempt be made to talk peace first. The people agreed, and sent five men with him to meet the Tswana and find out what their grievances were.

At the talks, the Tswana chief told them he only wished to discuss peace and cooperation. In reply, William and the local Griqua leaders asked the Tswana to return stolen cattle and seek to live in peace among themselves and with other groups. They would be welcome to come to Klaarwater to discuss their needs, they added. This action defused the tension, at least for a few months.[65]

On another occasion, when an attack by a large band of marauding Tswana seemed imminent, a similar peace party was sent out. William urged the people to pray for God's protection. He also made clear that they would defend themselves if attacked at any of their settlements, but this should be done only as a last resort. They were to use every means possible to maintain peace, he stressed.

They later learnt that the Tswana had been on the point of launching an attack when a sudden and violent argument broke out among them. Some had wanted to attack Klaarwater, while others had felt they should not attack.

That night, William and Johanna knelt together in prayer.

"Oh Lord, we praise You for Your gracious intervention on our behalf," they prayed. "You have heard our prayers and the prayers of the people. Give us peace and enable us to go forward in our work of proclaiming Your gospel to the poor heathen in these remote parts. How we long for the day when the gospel would so affect all the peoples of this part of Africa that peace and harmony would drive away fear and conflict. Amen."

Southern Africa in the 1800s was a cauldron of clashing cultures. William and Johanna represented two of those cultures, British and Dutch, but they were also well aware that they were representatives of a spiritual kingdom that transcended all cultures. Their loyalties could not be to their own 'white' culture, even though many equated 'civilization' with things European. Though almost totally cut off from events in far-away Europe, William and Johanna knew that Europe, too, was caught up in conflict. They knew enough about sinful human nature to know that all men and women, whichever culture they came from, needed the life transforming grace of God. They longed for peace and reconciliation to be passed down through succeeding generations.

Despite all the difficulties facing them, the Andersons and their colleagues gave themselves to the work of preaching and teaching. Jansz had decided to join them and was proving a most valuable helper. He was a friendly, likeable young man with a ready sense of humour.

William did most of the preaching and during the church services, people listened with eager attention. Although the services were carefully planned and formal, there was often spontaneous singing and individuals would stand up to speak. One time,[66] a Korana, his voice trembling with emotion, said in broken Dutch:

"I want to tell Mijnheer Anderson we is all very grateful for them is come to bring us the gospel. Our life now very much better, very much happier than before he come. Why? It is love that come to us. Love has change us. God love us people, this change our heart and bless our families."

Heads nodded in agreement. Many of them obviously loved the missionaries. William looked at Johanna and they both wiped away tears.

The two were especially emotional and excited, for Johanna was pregnant with their first child. As the time came near for her to give birth, William grew increasingly apprehensive. They prayed that everything would go well.

Just after midnight, in the early hours of 3 October 1807, Johanna went into labour. William did all he could to encourage her and remained kneeling by her side, both of them falling asleep in between the contractions. As the contractions became more frequent, there was nothing William could do but hold Johanna's hand and wipe the beads of sweat from her forehead with a wet cloth. Mrs Kramer and a Griqua mid-wife were called.

Finally after some twelve hours, the first gasp of breath and the cry of a newborn child was to be heard. Johanna soon fell asleep from exhaustion, but an overjoyed William found new energy, and it was not long before the whole of Klaarwater knew of the birth of little William Bartholomew, named after William's father and Johanna's father.

October 1807 proved to be a particularly joyful month for the Andersons. Apart from the birth of their son, it also saw Klaarwater's first baptisms. Those baptised were the two interpreters Piet Pienaar and Piet Goejeman; Andries Waterboer, the young Griqua leader who was an outstanding student and who had a good grasp of biblical truth; and Old Barend, Old Solomon Kok, Jan Mechiel, Ian Kok, Willem Fortuyn and his wife Mary, Nicolas Barends and Klaas Barends. It was a joyous occasion for the young church.[67]

October also saw the ordination by William of his two colleagues, Kramer and Jansz. The ordination service was a solemn occasion, attended by well over 300. William preached on Matthew 28:19-20 – "Go into all the world and preach the gospel."

With deep conviction, he said:

"It is this Great Commission that we seek to obey. No matter the slowness of the work, or the danger to life in such unsettled times and such remote parts, it is a privilege to be agents of the glorious gospel of grace and peace. This is our calling."

Grace and peace were rare and precious commodities then, as they are today.

---

[63] CWM/LMS/05/02/02/012, Anderson writing late November, 1807

[64] CWM/LMS/05/02/02/011, Anderson Journal, November, 1806

[65] CWM/LMS/05/02/02/012, Anderson Journal, March, 1807

[66] CWM/LMS/05/02/02/013

[67] CWM/LMS/05/02/02/013, Anderson Journal, October 1807

Arrivals and Departures

"How can I ever thank you all enough! You've been so good to me and the children." Mrs Kok spoke from her heart. She had stayed in Klaarwater a year and eight months following the murder of her husband Matthias.

"We will miss you. You have been like a sister," replied Johanna, as she, William, Jansz and several others gathered to say their farewells to Mrs Kok and those escorting her to the Cape.

It was II August I808. As was the case when anyone travelled to the Cape, Mrs Kok was entrusted with a wad of letters.[68] There was no other postal system. There were letters for friends in the Cape and in England, including directors of the LMS. Jansz had also written to his missionary society in Rotterdam.

Both Jansz and William had been working hard on finishing their journals for Mrs Kok to take to the Cape. William did not enjoy keeping a journal but as it was something the LMS directors requested, he did his best to oblige. There was also a letter for the Kramers, who had returned to the Cape soon after Kramer's ordination, several months earlier. Both William and Jansz missed their colleague.

Mrs Kok's departure meant that Johanna would be the only white woman left at Klaarwater. But this thought hardly crossed her mind. This was now home, and she enjoyed close friendships with many of the women. Her knitting and needlework class was always well-attended and a lot of fun.

Indeed, with almost 800 men, women, and children living in Klaarwater, life was seldom dull. There was always much to be done. The day school was attended by about ninety children and teenagers, while the Sunday worship services had about 360 adults. They packed the stone school house, and at times, there were as many people standing outside as there were seated inside.[69]

William and Jansz now shared the preaching and teaching. One Sunday, William was preaching on the 73rd Psalm.

"It is but folly to look with envious and jealous eyes on those who get rich by plundering and murdering others. Theirs is no real prosperity," he said. "Have you not yourselves seen how often those who gain riches through plundering others, after the same manner, have their riches taken away? When we see things from God's perspective, when we spend time in His presence, we begin to see things as they really are. We see the true end of the wicked and the true blessing of following God's ways."

William loved the Psalms. As was his custom in his preaching, after expounding the chosen passage of Scripture, he would try to apply it to the circumstances and needs of the people.[70] At the time, they were facing the threat of attack from marauding bands of Tswana.

He said,

"It would be the greatest wisdom, and would give us unbounded comfort, were we to know as the Psalmist did, the truth and power of these words - 'Whom have I in heaven but Thee?' What shall we say to these things that we hear? Shall we be discouraged? Shall we give up our confidence? No, that would be denying our profession of faith."

William's voice quivered with emotion as he continued: "They may rage and seek to attack us but if God be for us, who shall be against us? Let us trust in God who has given us this promise and many more in Jesus Christ."

William longed for a deep and powerful work of the Holy Spirit among the people. Though the missionaries found much encouragement in their work, by the end of September 1808, they had baptised only twenty adults and about forty children. In a letter to London the year before, William had written,

"Oh pray for us that the Word of our adorable Redeemer may be accompanied with a divine power and energy."

He and Jansz were still waiting for an answer to that prayer.

They had also been waiting for news of the Kramers. Finally, in October, they got a message from Kramer saying that he would not be returning until the situation seemed more peaceful. In Tulbagh, the Kramers had heard news of the on-going threats of attack against Klaarwater and were uneasy about returning. William felt the reports had somehow got exaggerated. Things in fact seemed more peaceful, for the present at least. They had also had soaking rains and had made good progress planting the new crops.

In mid-November, the Klaarwater community had several unexpected visitors.

An expedition, sponsored by the Cape government and led by a Dr Cowin and a Mr Donovan of the 33rd Regiment, arrived with four wagons. The expedition, or Commission, as it was called[71], consisted of a Colonist guide, two English soldiers and several Khoikhoi, some of whom were soldiers in the so-called 'Hottentots' Regiment'.

Cowin and Donovan had a letter for William, signed by the Governor, that requested every assistance be given the Commission. They were hoping to travel north through Tswana country before crossing eastwards to the coast in Mozambique. The Commissioners were very happy when some of the Griqua, including two of the leading men in the Klaarwater community, Ian Kok and his close friend Piet Goejeman, agreed to accompany them, at least part of the way. Some of the Griqua spoke reasonable Tswana and knew the country well.

Edwards, the missionary trader who had clashed with Kitcherer, also turned up in Klaarwater, having just been in Tswana territory. He also agreed to go with the Commission, for at least two or three weeks of their journey.[72] He too knew Tswana country quite well. Edwards' travel-weary wife and children remained in Klaarwater.

When Edwards and most of the Griqua finally returned in early January 1809, William was surprised to find that Ian Kok and Piet Goejeman were not with them.

"Where are Piet and Ian?" he asked.

"They agreed to continue with the Commission on their forward journey to Mozambique," said one of the men.

William felt uneasy. Later he said to Johanna,

"I know Piet and Ian will be a great help to the Commission and they will no doubt be an influence for good, yet we sorely miss their faithful service in Klaarwater. I must not, however, complain, for who knows – they may be of great use to the Master in the unexplored places to which they travel."

Little did William know that he would never see them again. Mystery was to surround the fate of the Cowin Donovan Commission.

---

[68] CWM/LMS/05/02/02/013, Anderson Journal, August, 1808

[69] CWM/LMS/05/02/02/014, Notes added on end of Anderson Journal, October, 1809

[70] CWM/LMS/05/02/02/013, Anderson Journal, July 1808

[71] Theal, George McCall: History of South Africa Since September 1795, Vol 1,
Cambridge University Press, originally published 1908, p.169.

[72] CWM/LMS/05/02/02/013, Anderson Journal, November 1808

CHAPTER 14:

Good News and Bad News

"My darling, I am concerned for your safety." William looked lovingly at Johanna. "Little Willie has not been well and now that you are expecting again, you need to be extra careful."

It was getting late and the flickering light from the candle that stood between them on the table lit up their faces. As was their regular habit, they had been reading the Bible together and were about to pray before turning in for the night.

"I know Brother Jansz feels we should be the ones to go down to the Cape, William, and I am concerned for Mother." Johanna paused as if her thoughts were momentarily far away. "How I'd love to see her again!" she sighed before continuing, "She's not getting any younger."

The tears in her eyes reflected the light from the candle. William understood how his wife felt, having lost both his parents and, in coming to Africa, having left behind all his friends and relatives in England.

Swallowing as she fought to control her emotions, Johanna continued,

"William, dear, I know the Lord is with Mother in Cape Town and she is happy for me to be here with you. Despite all the dangers that threaten us, I know the only thing that matters is the will of God and if He wants us here – this is where I want to be."

William squeezed her hand. He knew she meant it, and he admired her courage and faith.

Life in Klaarwater had been getting increasingly unsettled. If it was not the threat of inter-clan feuding among the Tswana just to the north, it was rumours of marauding Xhosa from the east. Some of the Griqua and Korana who had settled at Klaarwater and at Kloof began to talk of resuming their roaming lifestyle so that they could protect their cattle and sheep as well as the lives of their wives and children, more easily. Jansz was ready to move with them, if it became necessary, but he knew William was no longer in a position to do so, being a married man with a small child and a pregnant wife.

William and Jansz discussed the need for one of them to go to the Cape to sort out their affairs. They were in need of all kinds of supplies and it would also be a chance to try to allay the fears of their supporters and friends, and to seek advice from the authorities. They also had one of Dr Cowin's wagons, which had come back with Edwards and was half full of things the expedition had collected, such as animal skins and horns. These needed to be taken to the Cape.[73]

In mid-March, a group of church members came to see the Andersons and Jansz. They felt William and Johanna should leave as soon as possible before a large group of marauding Tswana returned from attacking another Tswana clan to the east of Klaarwater.

The people in Klaarwater had always been reluctant to lose the 'protection' afforded by the presence of their teacher. They knew that the Tswana had a great respect for William who was known as a man of peace. The Tswana were also aware of the part William and his colleagues had played in bettering the lives of the thousands of Griqua and Korana living in the settlements north of the Orange River.

But now, many Klaarwater residents felt it was too dangerous for William and Johanna to stay on. William did not want anyone to think he was deserting his people. However, as the church members had come in such earnestness, he began to feel much more at ease about going to Cape Town.

"William, I think this is the leading of God," said Jansz. "I too believe it is right for you to make the trip."

William and Johanna began to prepare for the long journey. Within days, they were ready to leave Klaarwater.

They knew that crossing the Orange River would not be easy. Memories of the near-disaster involving the Edwards flooded William's mind. When he saw their wagon carrying Johanna and their son Willie finally make it through the worst section of the rushing water, he threw up both hands in relief.

"Thank You, Lord! Thank You!" he cried out.

He followed on a raft pushed across by three Khoikhoi. He had decided not to travel in the wagon with Johanna so that the swimmers could direct all their attention to her and their little son if needed.

Their onward journey was blessed beyond all their expectations. They had plenty of water, as it had been raining, and the Karoo looked resplendent, sprouting with new life. The San they met along the way were all friendly, and they had no trouble from Tswana or Xhosa. Little Willie travelled well, as did pregnant Johanna. They arrived in Cape Town almost exactly two months to the day after leaving Klaarwater. It was Thursday, 19 May 1809.[74]

Cape Town was cold and wet, but the wood fire and delicious Schonken food soon warmed them up. Best of all was the fresh baked bread and the mutton stew. Mrs Schonken was delighted to see, at long last, her first grandchild, and was excited at the prospect of a second. In fact, five weeks later, she would hold in her arms her second grandson, Johannes.

The Andersons also had a happy reunion with Johanna's younger sister, Maria. She had recently married Johannes Seidenfaden who, like William, was a missionary. He had been working in extremely difficult circumstances among the Namaqua people in the arid country north of the Colony, south and west of Klaarwater. Seidenfaden was later to cause great heart-ache to Maria and her family, but in those happier days none of them were aware of the scandals to come.

Mrs Schonken was a brave and godly woman. She was very supportive of her daughters and proud that they were involved in missionary work. Not many in the Cape, even among regular church-goers, had any interest in such endeavours.

The day after arriving in Cape Town, William went to meet the Governor, the Earl of Caledon, taking along Dr Cowin's and Donovan's journals, as well as the items collected by the expedition. The Governor was delighted to meet William and the two men spent more than an hour in animated conversation. Lord Caledon seemed genuinely interested in all William had to tell him.

The following Monday, William and Johanna were invited to dine with the Governor at the Castle. It all seemed a long, long way from Klaarwater, what with the magnificent furniture and glowing chandeliers, the shining cutlery and precious china-ware, the sumptuous food and refined conversation. Lord Caledon repeatedly assured William of his willingness to offer all possible assistance and protection.[75]

More dinners followed with Admiral Bertie and other officials, and William was encouraged to present a written memorandum outlining his requests to the Governor. This he prepared with great care.

The memorandum contained an account of how his work was started and developed, and then William made six requests.

His first request was for his work to be given official recognition and the promise of protection, should it be necessary.

The second was for his people to be accorded the common privileges of any citizen when they visited the Colony. William saw all people – whatever their language, the colour of their skin, their social standing or level of education – as being equal in the sight of God and under the law. At the time, this request must have been seen by many as revolutionary, but William saw it only as reasonable and in accord with the teaching of the Bible.

Third, William asked that the government recognise the right of his church members to have their children baptised, and that the names of their children be officially entered in church or government records in Cape Town.

Fourth, he asked to be allowed to teach his people to write as well as to read. For some unknown reason, teaching the locals to write had been forbidden.

Fifth, he asked the government to make available to the people supplies of medicine, which were very expensive and often of poor quality.

His final request was to be supplied with gunpowder for protection on the road and when in Klaarwater.

Later, at the suggestion of the Governor's Secretary, Alexander, and the Governor's Assistant, Christopher Bird, William also asked for a supply of farming implements and tools for carpenters and smiths.

The wheels of bureaucracy turned slowly for William, but the Governor's support was evident in the reply he finally received on 11 October.

Signed by the Governor's Assistant, it read:

"Sir,

His Excellency, the Governor, has directed me to return you his best thanks for the account you have transmitted to him of the Missionary Establishment at the Great River, and to congratulate you on the success which appears to have hitherto attended your very benevolent endeavours. His Excellency is convinced that the example shown by the gentlemen who have devoted themselves to this arduous service, will have the most beneficial effects in recalling the natives of those fine districts to habits of industry and regularity, without which it will ever be impossible to bind them in society. His Excellency will be extremely happy in giving every support in his power to such endeavours and will have great satisfaction in affording the members of your Institution protection and assistance, if they stand in need thereof, when they enter the Colony.

His Excellency considers that the object you have in view for registering the baptisms of the people belonging to your Mission will be best effected by your transmitting every six months a copy of your register to the Landdrost of Tulbagh, who will be instructed to lodge a copy to this office with his annual Ofgaaf return.

His Lordship sees no objection to your teaching your people the art of writing, and His Excellency has directed that a supply of 100 lbs. of gunpowder may be supplied to you for your defence from the Government Stores.

His Excellency has further desired a sum of 400 Rixdollars, to be expended in procuring such requests as you may deem most useful for your Establishment, leaving the selection of them to your discretion.

With my best wishes for your further prosperity and success, I have the honour to be,

Sir, Your most obedient Servant

(signed) C Bird, Colonial Secretary, Assistant to the Governor." [76]

William was delighted, as were the directors of the SA Society. William wrote detailed letters to the directors of the

LMS in London giving them all the latest news. He felt it was important to try to keep on good terms with the 'powers that be', even though his primary concern was for his people and their well being. He would find out one day that the relationship between the Colonial government and missionaries would not always be so congenial.

William and Johanna prayed about when they might return to Klaarwater. News from Jansz was not good. Savage fighting had taken place between the Tswana and other black groups, though after Jansz called a day of prayer for peace, a threatened attack against Klaarwater was miraculously averted.

With such uncertainties looming over Klaarwater, the directors of the SA Society advised William and Kramer to leave their wives and children in the Cape until the situation was more settled. Little Johannes was just three months old and Willie only two years' old. It was a painful decision to part, but William and Johanna felt it was best that he go back alone.

Kramer had already left Tulbagh and was waiting for William at the Roggeveld mountains. Some of their friends from Klaarwater had come down to the Cape to accompany William. They were now ten days from Cape Town and had reached the Hex River. William did not want to tell anyone, but he was feeling giddy and had a searing headache. He did not know it, but his face was as white as a sheet.

"Mijnheer Anderson! Mijnheer Anderson!" one of the men shouted as he noticed William about to faint. He tried desperately to catch him, but it was too late. William lost consciousness and collapsed in a heap on the ground.

---

[73] CWM/LMS/05/02/02/014, Anderson to LMS, 24 July 1809, written in Cape Town

[74] Ibid

[75] Ibid

[76] Details of Anderson's meetings with Lord Caledon - see Anderson letters to LMS July 24, 1809 and June 30, 1809; and C. Bird to Anderson October 11, 1809 - all in CWM/LMS/05/02/02/014. See also The Caledon Cape Papers (D2431) and Caledon to Castlereagh, Oct 16, 1809 (Theal, George McCall: History of South Africa Since 1795, Vol.1, 170-5).

Dr Johannes
van der Kemp

CHAPTER 15:

Delay

There was no way William could continue. He persuaded the men to go on without him, inform Kramer, and deliver all the items he had prepared for Jansz and the Klaarwater community. He managed to scribble letters to Kramer, who was still waiting at the Roggeveld, and to Jansz in Klaarwater.[77]

Deeply disappointed, he then returned to Cape Town. He knew he was in no state to continue north to Klaarwater.

Soon, however, he and Johanna were to face a far more devastating trial. On 9 January 1810, their first son, William, who had caught an unknown virus and had been ill for just a few days, died in their arms.[78]

William and Johanna were heartbroken. There were no answers to their question, "Why?" They could only hold onto their firm conviction that God was both sovereign and loving, and it gave them much comfort.

By March, William was very much better. A letter from Jansz told of how distressed the people in Klaarwater were when they received the news of William's illness.[79] William read Jansz's letter to Johanna.

"Nothing would pacify them till I read that part in your letter where you assured me and the people that if you were restored to health, and the Lord permitted, you would certainly return."

William found himself choking with emotion, but continued reading. "Things are much quieter here now with the Tswana, and the people have asked me to tell you on no account to return without Johanna." William looked up from the page and smiled at his wife.

Johanna smiled back.

"William, by God's grace, I will return to Klaarwater with you," she said. "I do not care what criticism we get from anyone."

Their many months of waiting in Cape Town were not wasted. William took the chance to get to know many of the English soldiers stationed at the Cape. Every day, groups of twenty to thirty men would meet and William would preach to them.

The recently-founded Bible Society in London sent out large numbers of Bibles and New Testaments to a local Christian merchant, Duncan, who asked William to help him distribute them. William got permission to sell them at half price (one Rixdollar each) to the delighted soldiers. They bought thirty copies immediately, and later, another hundred.[80]

In general, however, William and Johanna found an indifference towards spiritual things in Cape Town. Most distressing of all, it was often the Dutch ministers who seemed to be most cold towards evangelism and missionary work. They found government officials friendly, but the same could not be said for those heading church affairs. William wrote to London,

"Oh, when will that happy time come when narrow spiritedness will have an end?"

William held firmly to his evangelical faith but he was not narrow-minded. He even wrote to the directors of the LMS asking if some books could be sent out for the Reverend and

Mrs Flock, the senior minister in the Dutch Reformed Church in Cape Town. William hoped this would strengthen friendship and cooperation and "more incline Rev. Flock to defend and support missionary work".

William and Johanna specially enjoyed meeting the LMS' newest recruits, Carl Pacalt and Michael Wimmer, with whom they spent long hours together. William found them warm and zealous, and was most impressed with them.[81] He told them a lot about the Tswana, for whom he felt an increasing burden.

"You know, Carl," he told Pacalt one day, "they are a very numerous people and have hardly been touched with the gospel. I've told you about Kok and his murder, but sad to say, even Edwards did little but barter for ivory. The latest news is that he has bought a farm in the Colony. Oh, what an extensive field there is among the Tswana! I certainly hope to learn more of the Tswana language on our return north and hope to collect as much as I can in writing."

Pacalt listened intently, and expressed the hope that he might be allowed to help in Klaarwater or in reaching the Tswana. What he and William did not know was that their names and their work would one day be inseparably linked, but not in Klaarwater nor among the Tswana.

Despite their fruitful activity in Cape Town, William and Johanna felt more and more frustrated at being delayed so long. They were longing to return to Klaarwater. This desire was fanned into a blaze when they received a visit from two Griqua members of the Klaarwater Church, William's close friends Ian Hendrick and Ian Koesa. With them were four Khoikhoi, also from Klaarwater.

As William was still not fully restored, he and Johanna were not yet able to leave the Cape. When the men were about to return to Klaarwater, William and some friends gathered with them for prayer. It was a most moving time. Just as William began to lead in prayer, the men burst out sobbing. It so affected everyone in the room that before long, all were weeping and it was only with great difficulty that William completed his prayer.[82]

Though William was eventually pronounced fit enough to return north, their departure was further delayed because of a terrible drought in Klaarwater. Jansz had to shelve his plans to send a party down from Klaarwater to Tulbagh to fetch the Andersons. This further delay, however, meant that William was able to see his old friend James Read once again.

Over ten years had passed since William, Read, Tromp, and van der Lingen had arrived in Africa from England. Now, Read had come to Cape Town with Dr van der Kemp, the first LMS missionary to Africa, with whom he had been working in the far east of the Colony.

Both men had been writing about the cruel treatment of the Khoikhoi by so-called 'Christian colonists' in the area of Bethelsdorp. The Governor, Lord Caledon, was aware of these allegations and wanted to discuss the situation with Read and Dr van der Kemp. Hence their visit to Cape Town.[83]

"May the Lord give you both great wisdom," William encouraged them, "to speak and act in a way that glorifies God and results in much needed help for the Khoikhoi. I am sure you will find Lord Caledon sympathetic."

The three men got on well together as they discussed their respective work, and William valued the insights and advice he received from them. He introduced Read to the soldiers and got him involved in the preaching. Read later wrote to the LMS and described William as "a man of sound judgment and amiable piety."[84]

Dr van der Kemp, too, summed William up as "a very valuable missionary".

"If Mr Anderson has any deficiency," he told Read, "it is that he seems a little inactive."

But William was in fact the persevering, plodding type. If he had given the impression that he was a little laid-back, it was possibly because he had been ill and he and Johanna had been delayed in returning to Klaarwater. At no time, however, could he have been said to be inactive. While his months of waiting in Cape Town were difficult and at times frustrating, they were certainly not fruitless.

Dr van der Kemp, the oldest of the three men, would die unexpectedly later that year, on 15 December 1811, while still in Cape Town. It would be a great loss to the LMS, as the doctor had a brilliant mind and the energy of ten men. Few could keep up with him.

It was June 1811. At long last, after nearly two years, William and Johanna were packed for the journey north. They now had a ten-week-old daughter, Maria Elizabeth, born in Cape Town in late March. Her birth, coming after the loss of their first son, brought her parents great comfort.[85]

It was not easy having to say good-bye to their second son, Johannes, who was to stay in Cape Town with Johanna's mother. The decision to leave him behind had been made with great reluctance. There had been reports of several hundred armed blacks waiting at the Zak River, intent on preventing their return to the Orange River. Friends had urged William and Johanna to leave at least one of the children in Cape Town.

"It is irresponsible to risk not only your own lives but also those of your children. You can always fetch Johannes when things have settled down," they argued.

A few weeks earlier, on 25 April, about twenty Griqua men from Klaarwater, together with their wives and children, arrived outside the Schonken home. They caused quite a stir with their wide-brimmed hats, home-made short leather trousers, leather sandals and blue 'English jackets', which without exception seemed far too long and baggy. They were a happy group and jabbered incessantly. They had come with oxen and a wagon to fetch the Andersons and accompany them back to Klaarwater. William and Johanna were overjoyed to see them.

Also joining them for the journey was Englishman, William J. Burchell, who had asked if he could accompany the Andersons as far as the Orange River.[86]

While stationed on the island of St. Helena in 1806, the young botanist from London had met deposed Dutch governor Janssens and Henry Lichtenstein, who were en-route for the Netherlands following the British take-over at the Cape. It was Lichtenstein, together with the Landdrost of Tulbagh, who had given a glowing report about William following their visit to Klaarwater in 1805. Burchell had heard about William from Janssens and Lichtenstein and now, four years later he found himself in Cape Town with the Andersons.

Wanting to explore the 'inland' areas, Burchell spoke with William at length. Not having experience of trekking and fearing reports of 'bushman atrocities', he accepted William's offer to travel together to the Orange. Burchell would later become famous for his illustrated works describing his "Travels in the Interior of Southern Africa."

On 18 June, the Andersons together with their Klaarwater friends and Burchell left Cape Town.[87] Burchell's new wagon was so heavily laden that it often sank in the sand, and finally its shaft snapped, requiring two days' repair work. Once in Tulbagh, Burchell got another wagon and spread his load, making travel much easier. Burchell appeared to prefer his own company and that of his two dogs to his fellow travellers. He was far more interested in his botanical and artistic pursuits than in religion or even people.

In Tulbagh, the Kramers joined the party heading north.

With frightening rumours of what might await them at the Zak, there was now considerable apprehension in the air as they left Tulbagh.

"Were the rumours about armed and hostile blacks true?" they asked each other. "How was Jansz?" "What was the situation in Klaarwater?" These were just some of the many questions going through their minds.

---

[77] CWM/LMS/05/02/02/014, Anderson from Cape Town, 27 November, 1809

[78] CWM/LMS/05/02/02/015, Anderson to LMS, 30 June, 1810

[79] Ibid

[80] CWM/LMS/05/02/02/014, Anderson to LMS from Cape Town, 1809

[81] Ibid

[82] CWM/LMS/05/02/02/015, Anderson to LMS, 26 August, 1810 from Cape Town

[83] CWM/LMS/05/02/02/016; see also John Philip, Researches II, pp 444-7

[84] CWM/LMS/05/02/02/016, Read to LMS, 26 June, 1811

[85] CWM/LMS/05/02/02/016, Anderson to LMS, 17 June, 1811

[86] Burchell, William John: Travels in the Interior of Southern Africa, Vol I, first published 1822

[87] CWM/LMS/05/02/02/016

Klaarwater
Church

CHAPTER 16:

Death Strikes

It was early morning, 20 September 1811. The bell rang, echoing down the valley and soon a large, excited crowd gathered.

The Kramers and Andersons, had arrived late the previous evening. Not wishing to awaken a sleeping Klaarwater, they had greeted only the two Griqua captains, Adam Kok and Berend Berends, and their missionary colleague Lambert Jansz. While most had slept unawares, news of their arrival had begun to spread like wildfire through the settlement well before dawn. There was excitement in the air as more and more people gathered to welcome them back.

At the public meeting, held half-an-hour after the bell had been rung, Jansz spoke first and then William, followed by Kramer and the captains. William ended the meeting with a prayer, giving thanks for a safe journey. He also gave thanks for God's faithfulness to Jansz and the people during his and Kramer's absence. It was an emotional but joyous occasion.

Johanna and Mrs Kramer, with the help of two or three local women, busied themselves putting away the various stores they had brought with them from the Cape. Their helpers were neatly dressed in European-style clothes, a marked contrast from the traditional Khoikhoi attire that half of Klaarwater's population still wore.

Burchell and his men, Willems and Speelman, arrived ten days later, having spent time in the area of Rietfontein near the Orange River collecting botanical specimens. Speelman's wife had been cooking for them, but once in Klaarwater Burchell enjoyed many a meal with the Andersons and Kramers

The botanist, however, was not impressed with Klaarwater. He had envisaged it to be much more developed, but now, all he saw were about thirty spherical reed huts and a few simple stone dwellings. The school house was also made of reeds, though it was to be replaced by a new stone building that was being built.

The largest building in Klaarwater was the church, which Burchell described in his notes as "rudely built of rough un-hewn timber and reeds, covered with a thatched roof, and having a smooth, hard earthen floor smeared with cow dung". The walls were covered with whitewashed mud and the ceiling consisted of no more than rafters and thatch. There were no seats; most of the people would simply squat on the floor during services. There was a wooden pulpit raised on a low platform.[88]

Religion was a peripheral matter for Burchell. He had other priorities in life. Over the following months, he would often wonder about what motivated people like the Andersons, the Kramers and Jansz.

"What makes them love these people so much?" he asked himself. "Surely they are taking religion and philanthropy too far! I can't help feeling they are over-zealous. Can they really believe our religion and civilisation will ever penetrate these parts? Is it even relevant here?"

Burchell's questions reflected the attitude of many Europeans of that era, who were unable to distinguish between the gospel and 'civilisation'. By the latter they meant 'European culture and education'. William often bemoaned the fact that many whites who regarded themselves as Christians were simply 'pagan

Europeans' who needed converting as much as his beloved, half-naked 'heathen' Griqua and Korana.[89]

Burchell, nevertheless, found a growing admiration for the missionaries. He tried hard to concentrate when listening to their Sunday sermons, but it was not easy. It was not the sermons he found hard to take, but the smell. At times, the aroma, especially in hot weather, of 300 or more greasy bodies, sheepskin karosses, tobacco and a host of other smells, made him feel worse than sick.

Very little got past Burchell's observant eye without being recorded in his notebooks. He was impressed with the gardens, especially those of the missionaries. The constant flow of water from the various springs enabled them to grow potatoes, cabbage, French beans, peas, lettuce, onions, beet, cucumbers, pumpkins, calabash, musk melons, water-melons, millet, and maize. There were also peach, almond, fig, walnut and orange trees, and wheat was grown in the cooler season. The missionaries also had a few chickens and ducks.[90]

"I notice there are many cattle in the district," said Burchell one evening over a cup of rooibos or red bush tea, with William and Johanna.

William nodded.

"Our people supply hundreds of head of cattle each year to the Colony. In return they bring back wagons, horses and sheep as well as other items."

"How many animals, on an average, do people own?" asked Burchell.

"It varies considerably," replied William. "One of our men has 400 cattle, 1700 sheep and 300 goats. Others have 200 cattle and several have between fifty and a hundred."

"Some of the people are very poor," Johanna added, "and actually work for those who are richer."

Burchell ended up staying in and around Klaarwater for several months, taking a number of trips eastwards, as far as the confluence of the Orange and Vaal Rivers. By January 1812, however, he was eager to move on.

William and the others tried to discourage him from travelling north, which made him angry. Burchell thought they were against it because they wanted to open up the Tswana areas themselves, and did not want him getting in their way. He also blamed William for the fact that no one in Klaarwater seemed willing to accompany him. But William was cool to his plans only because he feared for Burchell's safety.

"Burchell, my friend," he pleaded, "you should not under-estimate the danger to your own life of your travelling with so much gunpowder. It would be a big temptation to those who might want it for themselves, not least that ruthless brigand, Afrikaner."

Reports had reached Klaarwater that Jager Afrikaner was once again pillaging among the Namaqua people. At the time, the notorious brigand was based further downstream on the Orange River near the Augrabies Falls.

"And you well know," continued William, "that the expedition of Dr Cowin ended in disaster. We cannot encourage any of our people to accompany you, should you insist on going north."

Later, Burchell would travel south-eastwards, ending up in Graaff-Reinet, before returning three months later to Klaarwater en-route for Tswana country.

Those months, while Burchell was in Klaarwater, were among the most difficult. Many of the people were sick and the Kramers too were struggling with poor health.

Then Johanna fell seriously ill. At one point, she became so sick that she could hardly speak; at times, she was only semi-conscious. To make matters worse, little Maria Elizabeth also fell ill.

William became more and more anxious. There seemed to be nothing he could do and they seemed to be slipping away from him. Pain and agony filled his heart as he knelt by the bedsides of his beloved wife and little daughter in silent prayer.

"O Lord, I feel helpless and I am helpless," he prayed. "I am unworthy of Your love and mercy, but I ask for the faith to trust my beloved ones into Your ever loving and wise care."

He had been weeping, but as he prayed, he found comfort rising in his heart. He knew God cared for Johanna and Maria more than he ever could.

Soon, Johanna and little Maria began to pull through. Overcome with relief and joy, William told Johanna over and over that he loved her and that the Lord had graciously spared her and Maria.

Not long after, however, the searing sorrow of bereavement struck Cornelius Kramer. His wife was the youngest among the missionaries. She was pregnant but had not been well. Without warning, she suffered a miscarriage, and her condition very quickly deteriorated. Within a few days, she was gone.

Her sudden passing was a great blow to the Klaarwater community, especially to her doting husband. Johanna and William were deeply grieved and shocked, but they did all they could to comfort and assist Kramer.

On 25 January 1812, two days after her death, a large crowd gathered for the funeral. William, Johanna, Kramer and Jansz, together with the Kramers' young son, walked in solemn procession behind the coffin which was carried by six Klaarwater men.

Mrs Kramer was buried on the side of the hill at Leeuwenkuil, not quite two kilometres from Klaarwater. She was the first white woman to be buried north of the Orange River.

Her death had a deep effect on William. He spoke about it with Johanna, Jansz and Kramer, and also in his messages to the people.

"Her sad passing," he told his colleagues, "calls loudly to us to be active in our work and be ready waiting for the coming of our

Lord. May her home-call make us more faithful in dealing with our own souls and the souls of those committed to our care."

He continued, "Personally, I have been rebuked for my indifference and lukewarmness and have been stirred to see more the importance of the work to which our gracious God has called us. May I labour with more zeal to promote the welfare of immortal souls. Oh, how I long to see the out-pouring of divine power and blessing in this place! Oh, that many more of our people would, through our preaching, come to see their own spiritual need and come to know the Lord Jesus!"[91]

Kramer remained in Klaarwater for several months after the passing of his wife. Eventually, however, he returned to the Cape.

Despite the impact of Mrs Kramer's death on so many, there seemed to be a decline in spiritual life at Klaarwater over the following months. Even the numbers attending Sunday worship seemed to be decreasing.

William, Johanna, Jansz and a handful of the local believers continued to pray for revival.

"Lord," prayed William, "may it please You through Your Spirit to breathe again among the dry bones, that we may live a more spiritual life and bear fruit to the glory of Your grace."

Would God hear their prayer?

---

[88] Burchell, William John: Travels in the Interior of Southern Africa, Vol I

[89] CWM/LMS/05/02/02/017, Anderson to LMS from Griquatown, 26 June, 1812

[90] Burchell, William John: Travels in the Interior of Southern Africa, Vol I

[91] CWM/LMS/05/02/02/017, Anderson to Hardcastle & Burder, 4 August, 1812

Queen Mahulu

CHAPTER 17

History In The Making

*M*olehabangwe lay dying. His wives and sons, as well as his chief counsellors, spoke in hushed tones.

As chief of the powerful Tlhaping, a grouping of several Tswana clans, Molehabangwe was feared and respected far beyond the borders of his confederation. His influence stretched from the Langeberg mountains north-west of Klaarwater to the Harts and Vaal rivers, 250 kilometres to the east.[92] The Tlhaping received tribute from the Tlharo, some Korana and other tribes.

Molehabangwe's strength was fading but he was still able to talk coherently.

"The elders and tribal leaders must hear my words. I have some instructions to give to them and to my son, Mothibi," he said.

Mothibi, a young and handsome thirty-six-year-old, was the powerful chief's appointed heir.[93] His mother was a Korana.

"My son, our people have suffered much at the hands of the White Brigand," Molehabangwe said, referring to the raids of Jager Afrikaner.[94] "And, we have suffered much at the hands of marauding Xhosa, but," he continued, "I see a worse threat to our confederation. It is Makaba of the Ngwatetse."

The chief spoke softly, and those gathered around strained to catch each word. They knew that the loyalty of the Rolong, a tribe living to the north, was in question. The Rolong were once strong allies of the Tlhaping, but were being drawn into a rival Tswana grouping under Chief Makaba.

"My son, when I return to our ancestors," said Molehabangwe, looking straight into Mothibi's eyes, "you must strengthen the alliance. You must build friendship with the Griqua captains along the Great River and with their 'teachers' in Klaarwater. There could be many advantages."

It was not the first time Molehabangwe had said such things. Mothibi and the Tlhaping elders knew that the Griqua had guns and that their trade with the south, particularly with the colonists in the Cape, seemed to have brought considerable benefit to the communities along the Orange River. Mothibi also knew and respected the Griqua captains, who had a reputation as good fighters. And he knew of William Anderson – 'the peace-maker who loves his people'. Both Mothibi and his father had on two occasions met Jansz, and had been impressed by the missionary's politeness and honesty.

It was a warm evening in March 1812. Chief Molehabangwe gasped for one last breath. Mothibi was the new chief.

While Mothibi did not forget his father's dying words, he was not sure about the wisdom of making friendly alliances with white men, despite the good reports about the Klaarwater missionaries.

Tswana medicine men had on several occasions, when in their demonic trances, issued dire warnings about the dangers of associating with the missionaries. The spirits of the ancestors would be angry, they said, and disaster would strike. Mothibi feared the powers he saw controlling the medicine men. When the spirits of the ancestors spoke, it was foolish to disregard their warnings.

Then as now, few made the distinction between, on the one hand, the liberating truth of the gospel and, on the other hand, the heresies of ethnic superiority and the doctrine of 'might is right'. Demonic forces try to smother the gospel and are happy to use any heresy to assist their efforts. Neither Mothibi nor the missionaries were to know that one day 'white' expansion, as well as inter-ethnic conflict, would rob both the Griqua and the Tswana of much of their land and power.

It was a full year later when Mothibi had a surprise visit by a friendly delegation from Klaarwater. He was away on a hunting trip when five wagons reached his sprawling capital of Latakkoo.

Latakkoo was located in a broad and beautiful valley, which was dotted with thousands of beautifully thatched huts each with its own enclosure. It was a place of much life and movement, the inhabitants engaged in activities such as sweeping floors, making fires, cooking, grinding maize, winnowing sorghum, plastering walls, carving wooden utensils, making pots, weaving baskets, and flaying hides for aprons, karosses and other items of clothing. All kinds of sounds filled the air—from the happy voices of children at play and adults at work, to the lowing of cattle and bleating of sheep and goats.[95]

The Klaarwater visitors had arrived after a ten-day trip. In the party was John Campbell, a director of the LMS who had come from England and was on an extensive tour of southern Africa. The short but stocky young Scot had already travelled all over the Cape, visiting LMS missionaries from Cape Town in the south-west to Bethelsdorp in the east. From Bethelsdorp he had travelled with James Read north to Graaff-Reinet where they met up with botanist Burchell, who had recently returned from a trip through Tswana country (having gone as far as the sand dunes of the Kalahari desert). Not long after Campbell and Read had arrived in Klaarwater, William and Jansz had spoken with them about their desire to see the establishment of a mission to the Tswana people, and so the visit to Mothibi's capital had been planned.

Others in the party visiting Latakkoo included William, Cornelius Kok and his son Adam and several other Klaarwater men. Some of the men's wives had also come, but Johanna, who was three months pregnant, had remained at home. Johannes, now just over four years old, and little Maria, just over two, had also not been well.

As William and his party unyoked their oxen from the wagons, they found themselves surrounded by a large crowd of curious onlookers. They were stared at and examined from every angle, as were their wagons and possessions. Soon shy curiosity turned into near pandemonium and members of the Klaarwater party got separated in the jostling crowd.

With some effort, they eventually managed to form the wagons into a circle, pitched a large tent and sat down to eat, their every move watched by thousands of pairs of eyes.

William looked around him. Some of the men carried long-bladed assegais, or short spears. Most of the women wore little more than short skirts made of animal hide, and were heavily adorned with copper earrings, ivory bangles and anklets, and necklaces made of seeds. The children were mostly naked, apart from amulets around their neck which were believed to protect against disease or accident.

After sunset, nine Tswana elders arrived and sat cross-legged on the ground in the tent erected by the Klaarwater delegation. Most senior among them were Salakutu and Malayabang, both close relatives of Mothibi, and Munameets, a chief counsellor. Another was Mampe, an old but still revered former general.[96]

Campbell's sense of humour, never far from the surface, got the better of him, and he whispered to William and Read, "By the looks of these fellows, if we dressed them in large wigs and gowns, like our English judges, they would look equally respectable."

"Do you want me to translate that?" responded William, trying to keep a straight face.

Campbell began to speak. "Honourable sirs, we are told that your worthy king, Chief Mothibi, is away and can only return after a few days."

William translated his words into Dutch, which were then translated into Korana by Adam Kok, and finally into Tswana by a local who understood Korana.[97]

The Tswana elders nodded.

"We hope to meet with Mothibi," continued Campbell.

"I have come from a far country, where the true God, the Maker of all things, is known. A long time ago, this God sent some men to Klaarwater and other parts of Africa," he said, pointing to William and Read, "to tell the people things to make them happier."

The elders listened politely, occasionally glancing at each other.

"We have heard," Campbell continued, "that the Tswana people are friendly, and so we have come to find out if you would be happy for us to send you teachers who might come to live here among you and tell you more about these things."

There was some discussion among the Tswana. Then Salakutu, the late chief Molehabangwe's brother, responded.

"We cannot give you an answer till Chief Mothibi returns. We will send men to inform him of your coming. You will have to wait."

This wait lasted two weeks, but the time was not wasted. In the meantime, the visitors learnt a lot about the people and culture of the Tswana – and without knowing it, made a deep and favourable impression on the elders and the people.

One afternoon, while still waiting for Mothibi's return, the Klaarwater delegation had an unforgettable visit from Queen Mahutu. The queen, a mother of three sons and two daughters, was in her thirties and ravishingly beautiful. She was bedecked in magnificent necklaces of multi-coloured beads which covered her otherwise bare breasts. In addition to a group of armed warriors, she was accompanied by four other women, including Mothibi's sister Sitisu, who was tall and regal in appearance, but younger than Mahutu.

Mahutu had come to ask the Klaarwater delegation to remain in Latakkoo until Mothibi returned. She had heard they were considering going away for a short side trip, and feared that Mothibi would be very angry if they were away when he got back. The delegation assured the queen that they would continue to wait, which appeared to bring her much relief.

Mahutu was fascinated by a letter William showed her. It was from Johanna and gave news of the family and of Klaarwater, and someone had brought it that day from Klaarwater. The queen was amazed that the squiggles on the paper could communicate information. The Tswana, as yet, had no written language.

"What is this?" she asked, pointing to the Bible that lay on their folding table. This prompted a discussion on the value of books and, in particular, the value of the Bible. The missionaries told her about the Creator God.

"We also believe in the great high God," said the queen, still eyeing the Bible every now and again. "We call Him Morima." Then she paused and, shaking her head sadly, added, "But we do not know Him. He is very far away from us." She then asked seriously, "Where is God? Is He under the earth or somewhere else? Will people who are dead rise up again?"

The missionaries tried to answer these and many other questions.

At one point, Campbell, who had a slight cold, pulled out a large handkerchief and blew his rather big and red nose. Much to his surprise it sent Mahutu and her entourage into convulsions of laughter. Campbell, who always enjoyed having a good laugh, decided to join them, even if he did not fully appreciate the reason for their mirth.

The queen and her sister-in-law were genuinely interested in all that they had heard that afternoon.

"They may have some strange ideas," Mahutu thought as later she reflected on the meeting, "but they seem good and sincere men with much wisdom."

Finally, after several days, Mothibi arrived. He came straight to where the Klaarwater delegation were encamped, but seemed to ignore them.

Tall and muscular, the chief looked a formidable man. He was clothed in leopard skins and had a string of carved "ivory teeth" strung around his neck. Accompanied by several fierce-looking bodyguards, all carrying assegais, he sat down with great ceremony. He was surrounded by the elders, who proceeded to give detailed reports of all that had happened in his absence. The visitors simply had to wait.

After having a private conversation with Adam Kok, Mothibi finally indicated he was ready to talk to the rest of the Klaarwater delegation.

"You may now bow and greet our king," said an interpreter.

"Mothibi O iss!" they chorused. It was the greeting they had been told to use.

No sooner had they given their well-rehearsed greeting than the chief got up and left. The Klaarwater delegation were told he would receive them later.

At sunset, Mothibi and the elders returned and sat down in the Klaarwater delegation's tent. The missionaries were told they could now speak.

"Your Highness," Campbell began, "I have a small gift as a token of friendship." They had been advised that such a presentation would be correct etiquette.

Mothibi remained silent, not even moving his head, as he opened the parcel. Inside was an ornate copper comb, a silver chain, and a mirror. He proudly stuck the copper comb in his hair and looked at his reflection in the mirror.

"I don't know how I will shave in future," whispered Campbell to his colleagues. The mirror was from the lid of his shaving box.

Mothibi now spoke for the first time.

"You would have been perfectly safe coming on your own without Captain Kok and his friends. I would also have received you had you not brought any gifts." Mothibi paused then continued, "Captain Kok, you must consider Latakkoo as much your home as you consider Klaarwater your home."

"I am truly honoured, Chief Mothibi," Adam Kok replied with a smile and a bow.

Campbell proceeded to explain their mission to Mothibi.

"I have been sent a journey of four moons over the Great Sea," he said, "from the same country as Mr Anderson and Mr Read, in order to see how they are acting towards the people. They were sent to bring the teaching of God to the nations of Africa. Those at Klaarwater and also the Korana people have been glad to receive their message. We come now to ask your permission to send teachers here also."

Mothibi listened, then shook his head. "My people have no time for their instructions," he replied. "They have to attend the cattle, dig, sow and reap the fields, and do much else. Besides, the things you teach are contrary to all our customs."

"Your highness, may I briefly explain what we do teach?" replied Campbell respectfully.

"Of course. Please proceed." Mothibi seemed interested.

Campbell spoke of God, of creation, and of Christ coming to die for the sins of the world. Then, pointing to William's Bible, which happened to be on the table, he said, "This book contains all that we would tell the people. After our teachers have learnt your language, they will take what is in this book and put it into the Tswana language."[98]

Mothibi shook his head in disbelief.

William, seizing the opportunity, stood to his feet clutching a few sheets of paper. On them he had written the names of Mothibi's predecessors, his uncles, wives, brothers, and children.[99] William read these out loud and said, "Chief Mothibi, your language can be written down, even as English or Dutch can be written down."

Mothibi was amazed but obviously pleased with William's performance. He smiled for the first time.

Campbell went on to assure Mothibi that education and the teaching of the gospel would in no way prevent people from working.

"We will only teach those willing to be taught," he added, "and will in no way interfere with your government. The people must be free to accept or reject what is taught to them. We simply seek your permission to send teachers and would ask for your protection."

It was at this point, while Mothibi and his counsellors were discussing Campbell's requests, that Read whispered to Campbell, "Wouldn't it be wonderful if all the prayer friends in England could see what incredible things are happening here tonight?"

It was the first Monday of the month – the very day that supporters of the LMS in London and those serving overseas gathered to pray for the progress of the work. Clearly, their prayers were being answered.

Mothibi cleared his throat. His demeanour showed he was going to say something important.

"Send teachers," he said, "and I will be a father to them."[100]

He then stood up, shook hands with each of the Klaarwater delegation, and disappeared into the night.

[92] Legassick, Martin C., The Politics of a South African Frontier: The Griqua, the Sotho-Tswana and the Missionaries, 1780-1840, Basler Afrika Bibliographien, Basel, 2010, p 38 (originally a dissertation presented to the University of California, Los Angeles, 1969).

[93] Ibid

[94] Ibid, pages 70-74; and also Moffat, Missionary Labours, Chapters V-VIII.

[95] CWM/LMS/05/02/02/018; and Campbell, John, Travels in South Africa, Black & Parry, London, 1815, Chapter XVI pp 253-260. See also Burchell, Travels, II

[96] Details of events described in this chapter can be found in Campbell, Travels in South Africa, chapters XV to XIX, and William Anderson's letters and reports, CWM/LMS/05/02/02/018.

[97] Campbell, Travels, p 223.

[98] The author is in possession of William Anderson's Bible.

[99] Campbell, Travels, pp 283, 284.

[100] Campbell, Travels, Chapter XIX, p 287

Klaarwater

CHAPTER 18:

Momentous Decisions

The historic significance of the visit to Mothibi and the Tswana was not missed by William and his colleagues. John Campbell was so excited he could hardly sleep. He wrote at length to his fellow directors in London, adding,

"I cannot help wishing I could throw this letter to the other end of the Atlantic that it might land in the midst of the directors next Monday evening at the Old Swan."[101]

Campbell was a visionary, and could see the potential of reaching many other large tribes that spoke languages closely related to Tswana.

"The language appears to be relatively easy, having none of those claps with the tongue which the Korana and Hottentot languages have," he wrote. "A missionary such as Mr Morrison could learn and begin to translate in six months."

Campbell was referring to Robert Morrison, the first Protestant missionary to China, a gifted LMS linguist who was at the time busy translating the Bible into Chinese.[102]

Campbell suggested that after the Bible was translated into Tswana, multiple copies could be made by copying by hand from the original. Young Tswana men could then be sent around to read the Word of God to the people.

He wrote: "Each of these travelling readers would be a John the Baptist to preaching missionaries who would come after them. In this way, the truth might travel up the unknown regions of Africa faster than many could believe."

Campbell's vision for the Tswana was not an empty dream, although it would take a few years before teachers could come to learn the Tswana language and begin to translate the Bible.

The first to do this were Robert Hamilton and Robert and Mary Moffat, who lived among the Tswana at Kuruman in the early 1820s. Located a little south of Latakkoo, Kuruman had a strong spring and was close to where Mothibi later moved his capital.

Moffat's work in translating the Bible into Tswana placed him alongside other great Bible translators such as William Tyndale and Martin Luther in Europe, John Eliot in North America, William Carey in India, and Robert Morrison in China.

Campbell's visit to Klaarwater also had a significant impact on the Griqua community, and led to some momentous decisions.

One was the changing of the name of the inhabitants of Klaarwater to 'Griqua'. Up until then, they had been called 'Bastards'. Though there had been some inter-marriage with both Europeans and San, the Griqua were largely Khoikhoi in origin, having descended from a Khoikhoi clan called the Grigriqua.[103] While they had lost most of their original Khoikhoi language and many of their customs, they had, especially since settling in Klaarwater, felt a clear sense of kinship.

The change of name strengthened the Griqua identity, for it meant that the original 'Bastards' from the Colony were now grouped together with the indigenous Korana, Nama and even some San. The captains, Adam Kok and Berend Berends, were very happy with the change of name.

They also decided to call Klaarwater by a new name – Griquatown.[104]

Another result of Campbell's visit was the formal acceptance of a set of thirteen laws that codified various misdemeanours that were already considered offences by the people. The punishments varied from execution for convictions of murder, to flogging, hard labour or restitution for stealing or harming property or livestock. These regulations were to be enforced by nine magistrates elected by the people.[105]

Early in August 1813, Campbell and Read prepared to leave for Namaqualand. They had been deeply impressed by all they had seen and experienced in Griquatown.

"This place is a light to all around," Campbell told William and Jansz. "It has refreshed me beyond words to see evidence of God's working in the lives of so many of the people here. To see a man building a house who formerly lived under a bush; another keep cattle for breeding who formerly devoured them as fast as he could get them; another becoming mild and gentle and affectionate who formerly resembled a lion or tiger; another speaking about the things of God who formerly seemed to have the mind of a beast . . ." Campbell paused, then continued with conviction, "you must feel that all your sacrifice over the past years has been abundantly worthwhile."[106]

"You are right, Brother Campbell, we do," replied William, "but let it be known that whatever has been accomplished is God's doing. And furthermore, we long for much more evidence of His work here. So many remain as yet untouched."

Such a response to praise, was typical of William Anderson, and he meant it sincerely.

Campbell and Read had themselves been well received in Griquatown, and everyone was sad to see them leave. One young woman was particularly sad – Jansz's beautiful bride

Esther, the daughter of one of Griquatown's leading Christians, Piet Pienaar.[107]

Esther had spent many happy hours with Read's Khoikhoi wife, who had accompanied her husband from Bethelsdorp. Mrs Read and Esther had a lot in common, both having married white missionaries. There was no prejudice against such unions in Griquatown, but many colonists in the Cape were opposed to whites marrying 'people of colour'. Both Read and the late Dr van der Kemp had been severely criticised for marrying non-European women.

Many months before the Campbell visit, Jansz had told William of his growing love for Miss Pienaar and asked for his advice, and William had discussed it with Johanna. They knew Esther.

"Esther is not only a very lovely young woman but also a truly devoted Christian," said Johanna. "She will make a wonderful wife for dear Mr Jansz."

"I agree," said William. "Her father, Piet, is one of my dearest friends. When I first came to live among the people along the Orange River, he was one of the earliest to believe and was the one who never left my side when I was so close to dying. To my mind, colour of skin should have nothing to do with how we regard people. Piet's daughter is one of our best young people, quite apart from her good looks."

When William and Johanna saw that the relationship might indeed lead to marriage, they gave the young couple their full blessing.

The wedding was a very happy occasion. Esther and Jansz had a very loving relationship, and she quickly became a great support in his work. She was popular with the young and also got on well with the older people. In addition to Dutch, she spoke fluent Tswana as well as Korana.[108]

A few months after the marriage, Esther confided in Johanna that she thought she was pregnant. Johanna hugged her and whispered back that she, too, was expecting a child.

Now, four months later, Johanna and Esther stood together, arm in arm, in the cold evening air as they waved good-bye to Mrs Read and the rest of the Campbell party. It was full moon as the wagons finally headed south out of Griquatown.

---

[101] CWM/LMS/05/02/02/018

[102] Horne, Silvester: The Story of the London Missionary Society, London, 1908, p 107.

[103] Briggs, Roy and Wing, J, The Harvest and the Hope, United Congregational Church of Southern Africa, Johannesburg, 1970, p 25.

[104] CWM/LMS/05/02/02/018

[105] Ibid. See also Legassick, M.C., The Politics of a South African Frontier: The Griqua, the Sotho-Tswana and the Missionaries, 1780-1840, Basel, 2010, pp 93, 94.

[106] Campbell, Travels, Chapter XIX

[107] CWM/LMS/05/02/02/018, Read to LMS from Klaarwater, 29 July 1813

[108] Ibid

CHAPTER 19

Breakthrough

*U*nusual things were taking place in Griquatown.[109] The Andersons were having an increasing number of visitors, almost all of them in considerable distress.

"Oh, Mijnheer Anderson," groaned Willem Berend, "I never think about anything but hunting. It fills my dreams. Even in church I cannot concentrate and am really pleased when the preaching is over. I have found myself hating anything to do with you and your God."

Berend began to sob, as William laid his hand gently on his shoulder.

"Mijnheer Anderson," Berend continued, trying to control himself, "now I am convinced I must have the Lord Jesus or I will be lost forever."

Another evening, a young lady, Leintje Goejeman, came to see the Andersons. No sooner had she sat down when she burst into tears.

"My sins are too many, too many. I shall be lost!"

"Dear Leintje," said William reassuringly, "You might think you will be lost but Jesus is a great Saviour, able to save anyone – including you."

"But Mijnheer, I have listened to the devil. Before, when I knew I should ask for Jesus to save me, something said to me, 'Stop it! You are too young. You have no sins. I will help you.' Mijnheer Anderson, I listened to this voice. I now know it was the devil. Oh, I shall be lost!" Again she started to weep.

Johanna put her arm around Leintje and together, she and William spoke of how she might find forgiveness and peace.

There were many others who felt this kind of conviction. One woman told them she often dreamt that she was lying at the edge of a deep pit into which she was about to fall.

A constant stream of people were coming to the missionaries and to some of the local Christians for help and counsel.

Some who used to oppose the missionaries changed completely.

One of them was Jacob Kloete, who had long been one of Griquatown's most notorious characters. A ring-leader among the youth, he was known for his drunken and immoral behaviour. It was Kloete who had been flogged for raping a nine-year-old girl. People were afraid of his wild temper and ever-ready fist.

Much to the surprise of all, not least his friends, Kloete began to show respect towards William and Jansz, often even coming to chat to them about the Bible and related topics. He started attending meetings and seemed genuinely sorry for all the trouble he had caused the community.

One day a group gathered around William. One of the men said,

"I used to be most comfortable when at a distance from you, Mijnheer." William wondered what would follow. "But," the man continued with a broad smile, "now I can't get close enough!"

"Yes," said another man. "Many of us are amazed you have stayed with us for so many years. Now we know it is only the love of Jesus. He has given us the chance to continue to hear His Word, even when we despised it so much."

The people suggested that a weekly Testimony Meeting be started. It proved very popular, with crowds of both young and old attending regularly. Many spoke publicly of how God had got through to them, and everywhere in Griquatown one could hear people talking about 'spiritual things'.

Another young man, Andries Hendrick, who had been away for a few months, returned to Griquatown to find the 'revival' in full swing. He felt he had come into a new world.

"Everyone is speaking about Jesus," he complained. Soon, however, he too came under conviction and became a devout believer.

Often, when William was out in the corn fields, he heard people praying. Some were praying for themselves, others for their friends and family members.

Prayer meetings were popular, and many gathered to pray every night. Even the young people were inspired, and decided to start their own prayer meeting. One of the most zealous was fifteen-year-old Solomon Berends, son of Griqua captain Berend Berends. The young people also loved to sing, and the sound of their beautiful harmonies could be heard wafting across the valley during the 'revival' of 1813.[110]

William had always been slow to make great claims for the success of his work. He looked for more than outward profession, and was never quick to receive new church members.

He and Johanna could not, however, hide the joy and excitement they felt as they saw all that was happening. They knew it was a true work of God – something they had longed and prayed for. They saw real change in many church members, and were especially happy when some openly showed remorse at having treated the San and the Korana with contempt.

"We are guilty, brothers and sisters," said one at a prayer meeting, "of failing to tell the Bushmen and Korana about God's love for them."

This was followed by a most moving time of prayer, when one after another prayed with great earnestness for the San, the Korana and the Tswana. After this some of the men began to go out on Sundays to preach in nearby San and Korana villages.

In October 1813, William and Johanna took a sixteen-day trip to visit some of the more distant San and Korana villages. They were warmly welcomed as they visited the different family groups, hut by hut. William found intense interest whenever he preached to larger groups. After preaching in one San village, he asked some of the people what they thought of it all.

"I cannot say I like the thought that God will punish sinners," said one of the men.

"Well," responded William, "if a child is naughty, does its parent not have a right to punish the child?"

"If the son be grown up," responded the man, "the father would be afraid he himself might get beaten, but I admit a parent does have such a right."

"Well," said William, "God has the right to punish sin, but He loves us sinners so much that He gave His Son to die for our sins. If we believe this, we need not be afraid."

"I want to believe what you have told us," said the San seriously. All the others who had been gathered around listening nodded their agreement. They too wanted to believe.

By the time William and Johanna reluctantly left that village, they felt sure some had come to genuine faith. They left to the sound of San singing and praying together, which enthralled them.[111] When they were some distance away and no longer able to hear the San singing, they themselves began to sing.

In December, when Jansz and an obviously pregnant Esther, were visiting Griqua and Korana settlements south and east of Griquatown, they too found great interest among the people. On their return, they shared with the Andersons what had happened.[112]

"About twenty, mostly young folk, came to faith. The Holy Spirit was obviously at work," said Esther. "Many were seeking the Lord with tears."

"One really hardened opponent of the faith came with tears of repentance," added Jansz. "He begged me repeatedly to tell you, William, that he loved you and longed to see you."

"That is amazing, Lambert!" said William, himself fighting tears. He knew the man and had on more than one occasion been openly cursed by him.

The missionaries were not the only preachers. Berend Berends was particularly zealous in his support of the preaching and teaching in and around Griquatown. He often travelled the fifty kilometres down to Kloof, now re-named Hardcastle after an LMS director in London, where he and another local man, Peter David, would preach to the people there.

After one of his own trips to Hardcastle with Berend Berends, William excitedly told Johanna,

"I had not one minute to myself. There was a constant stream of one or other coming to speak to me about spiritual things. After visiting different homes, on my return to the wagon, I found a large number waiting for me, wanting to talk. Many repented in tears. It was amazing!"

Johanna poured William another mug of bush tea as he continued. "And dear Brother Berend is being greatly used by God. As you know, he speaks both Dutch and Korana fluently and he has led many Korana to faith. He and Peter David are obviously much loved by the people."[113]

And so the revival in and around Griquatown continued well into 1814.

With such spiritual breakthrough, it was surely only a question of time before satanic opposition would be felt. Indeed, there was a subtle but powerful counter-attack, and when it came, it came from unexpected quarters.

---

[109] CWM/LMS/05/02/02/018, Anderson Report for 1813
[110] Letters from Anderson and Jansz to LMS in London, CWM/LMS/05/02/02/018
[111] Ibid
[112] Ibid
[113] CWM/LMS/05/02/02/019, Anderson to Read, 18, February, 1814

CHAPTER 20:

Counter-Attack

*T*hough Griquatown was an oasis in an otherwise harsh and dangerous wilderness, life for a young family was never easy. Johanna was finding it hard to cope with the final days of her pregnancy, not least because fifteen-month-old Catherina and two-and-a-half-year-old Maria were both seriously ill.

Catherina, nicknamed Kitty, was their fourth child. Johannes, their oldest surviving child, was by now an active four-and-a-half-year-old. Christmas came and went, and on 30 December 1813, much to their relief, their third daughter was born safely. They called her Johanna Wilhemena.

Jansz and his wife Esther too were getting excited as the time for the birth of their first child was fast approaching. William had been visiting Hardcastle, and as he rode the last few dusty miles towards home, he wondered if there would any news. His horse also seemed eager to get home and broke into a gallop.

There was news. Esther was in labour, and both her mother and Johanna were with her. A most difficult and painful eighteen hours passed before she finally gave birth to a son on 28 January 1814.

But Jansz's joy was quickly overshadowed by his wife's suffering. She had found only temporary relief after the birth;

153

the pain in her stomach was excruciating, and she could hardly breathe at times.

Mustering all her strength, she whispered to Jansz,

"Lambert, I am afraid I cannot make it. I am dying, but please don't grieve for me, my darling."

Somehow she survived the night, and over the next few days managed to rally several times. Each time, however, she suffered a relapse and became weaker.

Early in the morning of 3 February, she called for William.

"Mijnheer Anderson," she said faintly but earnestly, "please pray for me, that I will be able to give up Lambert and my child into the Father's Hand."

A trickle of tears rolled down her pale cheek as she continued, "I do not think I will live, but I have no fear and have much happiness in Jesus, my dear Redeemer. The only reason I desire to live is for the sake of my husband and my child."

With great tenderness, William prayed for her, but his heart was aching.

"Thank you," she said with a smile, when he finished. "At times it crosses my mind that should God spare me, I would stand up in church and sing His praises at the top of my voice, but I have little hope of that."

She then began to pray, "Lord, if I die, please make my funeral a great blessing to all the Christians and also to those who are not yet converted. And Lord, please comfort my dearest husband, Lambert." She then began to sing 'Ja genade voor genade', 'Yes, grace upon grace'.

William left her bedside feeling he had been in the presence of a saint.

In the following days, as Esther grew weaker, never once did anyone hear her complain. On one occasion when Johanna was with her, she said,

"Oh, how my Saviour suffered for me! I dare not complain. All is mercy."

Early in the morning of 10 February, Esther died, a gentle smile on her thin but still beautiful face.

The whole church, as well as over two hundred others, attended the funeral.[114] William preached a short but powerful sermon at her grave-side and though many were moved to tears, there was a sense of triumph and hope throughout the service. Several believed as a result of the funeral, and were later accepted as members of the church.

Though Esther Jansz's death was a severe blow to the community at Griquatown, the revival of the previous six months continued unabated.

One Sunday afternoon, a few weeks after Esther's funeral, William preached a powerful sermon before a large and attentive crowd before baptising twelve adults. It was an emotional occasion, and people were visibly moved. Many said the meeting was too short, despite the fact that William had preached for almost two hours.

That same month, they began to administer the Lord's Supper every other Sunday. Previously, they had followed the Dutch practice of holding Communion only once every three months.

Unknown to them all, however, a far more serious attack was on its way.

Towards the end of March 1814, William received a letter. Dated 3 January, it bore the seal of the Cape government and had been sent from Tulbagh. William opened it hurriedly, and saw that it was signed by Colonel Reynolds on behalf of the current Governor, Sir John Cradock. Reading it as quickly as he could, he was shaken by its contents.

"This is dynamite! Surely Cradock can't be behind it," he thought. "There must be other forces at work."

William sensed this might be a 'spiritual' attack for into his mind came the Scripture, ". . . our struggle is not against flesh and blood, but against the rulers, against the authorities, against the powers of this dark world and against the spiritual forces of evil in the heavenly realms".[115]

The Cape government was demanding that William make sure all "deserters, criminals, slaves, (Hottentot, or Bastard)" who had escaped to the Orange should be returned to the colony.

In addition, he was to arrange for twenty youths between the ages of seventeen and twenty from Griquatown, to join the Cape Hottentots' Regiment. They were to serve for seven years and would be discharged and paid a lump sum of ten Rixdollars if an equal number were found to replace them. While serving, they would receive 'religious and secular education'.[116]

William was shocked because he knew the Governor had previously given warm support to the missionary cause.[117] He showed the letter to Johanna, then to Jansz.

"Brother Lambert, how can we possibly expect our people to take kindly to these unreasonable demands?" he said, looking at Jansz, then continued, "We are hundreds of miles beyond the furthest border of the colony, the vast majority of our people owe them not the slightest allegiance, and yet they wish to bring our people under their jurisdiction. It is an insult on top of all this to offer a paltry ten Rixdollars, one week's wages, after seven years of service – and only if others are found to replace them."

William knew that the latest demands by the Cape government would only add to his people's resentment over how the Khoikhoi in the Colony were being treated little better than slaves. Although the slave trade was supposed to have been abolished in 1807 [118], various laws enacted since then had only seemed to tighten control over the Khoikhoi. Read and other missionaries at Bethelsdorp had spoken out strongly against the ill-treatment of the Khoikhoi by some colonists. As a result Read and his LMS colleagues had faced strong opposition from some colonists as well as from the colonial government.[119]

Unknown to William, there were also rumours circulating in the Cape that he was encouraging Khoikhoi in the Colony to desert and join his institution at Griquatown. Some accused him of harbouring escapees from justice.

William discussed the matter with the captains, Berend Berends and Adam Kok, and on 24 March they called a public meeting. The atmosphere was tense as William read out the letter and explained its contents. He tried to remain objective and said it would be good to show respect for the Cape government.

"After all," he argued, "they have promised us free access to the colony for trade and have made gunpowder available from time to time."

Nothing William said, however, calmed the people's unhappiness with the governor's letter.

It was clear that no one would sign up to the Cape Hottentot's Regiment. Several men spoke, saying that while they had been happy to cooperate with the Cape government in the past, these latest demands were a threat to their freedom.

"I was born here," said one man, "and I refuse to leave my country."

William fully agreed, but tried not to show his feelings. He promised to write to the government explaining the position of the people. He knew he would be caught in the middle, even though his sympathies were with his people.

Not surprisingly, William's reply drew a swift and strongly worded response from the Cape government. The letter was signed by Mr C. Bird, formerly the Governor's Assistant but now deputy Colonial Secretary, on behalf of Lord Charles Somerset, who had succeeded Cradock as governor.

Dated 27 May, it reached William in Griquatown on 4 July 1814. It acknowledged that the LMS Institution headed by

William was outside the colonial border and "therefore not properly subject" to the Cape government, but went on to point out that William had "on every occasion received protection from the Colony."

The letter went on, "If you then wish that this protection should be continued to you, the condition imposed must be that . . . of contributing to the General protection. On the other hand, should you continue to refuse the aid required . . . then all communication and connection whatever will be considered as at an end between your Establishment and the Government of this Settlement."[120]

The future of William's work among the Griqua along the Orange River was now under threat. And it had come from some of his own countrymen, all of whom no doubt regarded themselves as both Christian and civilised. William felt they were neither.

---

[114] CWM/LMS/05/02/02/019, Anderson to Read, 18 February & to London 28 February, 1814

[115] Ephesians 6:12

[116] CWM/LMS/05/02/02/019; see also Horne, Silvester: The Story of the London Missionary Society, London, 1908, p 70.

[117] CWM/LMS/05/02/02/019. See also Philip, Researches II, 61-62.

[118] Abolition of the Slave Trade Act, 1807, British Parliament, passed on 25th March 1807.

[119] le Cordeur, Basil A: The Occupations of the Cape, 1795-1854, from An Illustrated History of South Africa, Jonathan Ball Publishers, Johannesburg 1986, p.82.

[120] Recorded in full in Anderson's correspondence with the LMS, CWM/LMS/05/02/02/019

Lord Charles Somerset

CHAPTER 21:

Heavy Blows

*N*ever before had so many of the workers of the LMS been able to meet together for prayer and to discuss their work. The August 1814 conference, held in the town of Graaff-Reinet, was hosted by Kicherer, with whom William had first travelled inland to the Zak River and who was then the minister in the town's Dutch church.

William had travelled down to Graaff-Reinet with his family and several leading members of the Griquatown church, including Ian Hendrick, Berend Berends, Peter David, and Andries Waterboer. At the conference, they were appointed as lay preachers, together with Jan Goeyman and Cupido Kakkerlak from Bethelsdorp.

One issue of particular concern at the conference was the demand of the Cape government regarding the recruitment of youths for the Cape Hottentot's Regiment. All were unanimous in their opposition to the government's demand. A letter would be written to the new Governor and signed by those in attendance.[121]

The tone of the letter, however, was conciliatory. While raising several issues, it focused on the situation facing William and Griquatown. It pointed out how precarious the work among the peoples north of the Orange was, and how sensitive they were to European expansionism. It pointed out that when William first settled among them, the people suspected him of having been sent by the Cape government to ensnare them. On more than one occasion they had planned to kill William. However, by their patient and loving labours, William and his colleagues had proved their integrity and gained the confidence of the people. The letter also said that William would visit Cape Town and provide any further information the Governor wanted. The letter concluded,

"We pray that every blessing may attend His Excellency's person and Government."

The missionaries' efforts to express their concerns tactfully and respectfully, however, were wasted. When the aristocratic and autocratic Governor, Lord Somerset, read their submission, he was furious.

A few weeks later, William and Johanna and their four children arrived in Cape Town. As usual, they stayed with Johanna's mother. Mrs Schonken had aged noticeably and her long hair, which she kept plaited and tied up in a bun behind her head, was completely grey. She had been ill, though she would live another thirty years, to the age of almost ninety-five.

William immediately made plans to visit the Governor at his residence. He was expecting fire-works.

The formal introductions were polite enough. William could not help thinking he would rather be with his poorly-dressed flock north of the Orange than in the leather-chair, chandelier luxury of the Governor's residence.

Lord Somerset seemed calm until he held up the letter sent by the missionary conference in Graaff-Reinet.

"Who do you missionaries think you are?" he said, obviously unable to suppress his anger. "What leads you to think you have the right to deliberate upon the orders of Government?"

"Your Excellency," replied William, "it is a sensitive matter and affects our very life and work."

"I am sure Mr Anderson can explain their situation, your Excellency," intervened the Colonial Secretary, Alexander. "I am sure he is eager to cooperate with us in the best interests of the Colony."

William was not sure he fully agreed, but said nothing.

The Governor, who seemed to have calmed down at little, resumed,

"Mr Anderson, you may not be aware of this, but there are very serious rumours circulating in the Colony concerning you and your Institution. I believe you now call it Griquatown."

"Yes, your Honour," William interjected, "I have been told of some of these rumours. They are all totally untrue."

William was asked to explain himself, which he did as politely as possible. There followed some detailed discussion.

Looking him straight in the eye, the Governor said sternly,

"Mr Anderson, I have to remind you that the Hottentots at the Orange are subjects of the British Government, as are all others within the borders of the Colony."

"Your Excellency, forgive me, but that is not true," William replied with a boldness that surprised even himself. "Most of those living at the Orange were there long before we came to Africa. The children of those among them who once did formerly live in the Colony, were all born at the Orange. Certainly all those of the age seventeen to twenty, who are being wanted for the Hottentot Regiment, were born there."

William was himself now quite angry. "When I first came to Africa, sir, few troubled their heads about the so-called Hottentot when they could buy a slave for one hundred to 300 Rixdollars. Now that the curse of slavery is removed, and there is a shortage of labour, the colonists wish to enslave the Hottentot."

The Governor was clearly annoyed with what William said, but listened nevertheless. He told William to continue.

"Thank you, Your Excellency," said William. "On the issue of the Government's request for soldiers for the Cape Hottentots' Regiment, I believe it is impossible to enforce, and it could lead to the total break-up of the settlement at Griquatown."

William explained that agriculture would cease, because the Griqua were the only people cultivating the land; the Korana mainly lived off their cattle, while the Bushmen depended on hunting and collecting wild roots.

"You should know, your Excellency, that as far as the Griqua are concerned, their independence is as precious almost as life itself," he said. "The land is settled and they have homes. They are strongly prejudiced against the colonists, and if you will forgive my saying it, sir, I believe they have good reason to be."

The Governor listened without saying a word.

William continued,

"My people have asked me, 'What have we done to forfeit our privileges? Have we made bad use of our guns?' No, your Excellency! I believe if force is used against our people and if the privileges hitherto afforded them, such as engaging in lawful trade with the Colony, are removed, the results would be calamitous. Our work would be destroyed and other nations, such as the Tswana, currently waiting eagerly for Christian teachers, could be turned against us also."

Then, seeing the Governor had had enough, William said no more.

"Thank you, Mr Anderson. No doubt we will be in touch again." Lord Somerset had other business.[122]

Over the next few months, William had further discussions with various officials, including Alexander and Bird, the deputy Colonial Secretary. He told them he wished to return to Griquatown as soon as possible and expressed the hope that the

Governor would back down on his demands. He heard nothing from the Governor himself until 16 November, when he was summoned to the Governor's residence.

"Are you ready to depart, Mr Anderson?" Lord Somerset asked, when William was seated.

"Yes, your Excellency. I am only waiting for your Lordship's answer to our appeal concerning the Government's demands."

"Mr Anderson, I assure you, you are free to leave, and at any time, may return to the Colony. I do not intend to use force with your people, but as they have refused me their assistance, I am unfortunately unable to offer them any assistance or protection."

William was relieved to hear this, though also worried.

"Your Lordship," he replied, "I sincerely thank you for declining to use force and for promising not to oppose our work. However, for me to lose the moral support of the government, to lose your approval and your favour, could seriously undermine my own position and authority, especially with those among our people who are more inclined to unruly behaviour."

"Well, Mr Anderson, that is too bad. I act purely from the principle of the matter." The Governor obviously had no more to say on the topic, and after a short, polite conversation on other matters, the interview came to an end.[123]

While in Cape Town, just prior to his final meeting with Lord Somerset, William had written to the directors of the LMS.

"The difficulties in which it has pleased the Lord to bring our station, will no doubt work together for good. Something of this kind was to be expected. If it may be a means of impressing the minds of our people with a deeper sense of the mercy of God toward them in sending His gospel there, and they become more active, more devoted, more spiritual in their walk and conduct and diligent in their various callings, it will be worth it all. I hope it will be a means of drawing us missionaries to more devotedness and activity, and teach us and the Society that it is not by power or by force, but only through the grace and Spirit of our God that we can go forward."[124]

William was not only concerned about the growing opposition of the government to missionary work. He was also distressed by the disunity he saw among the LMS missionaries.

Fellow Scot George Thom, who was based in Cape Town, for instance, had been scathing in his criticism of missionaries who married Khoikhoi women. He even had doubts about the white women born in the Colony and approved only of wives 'imported' from Britain or Germany.[125] William found he had much in common with Thom on issues such as slavery – Thom also opposed the trading in slaves that was continuing at the Cape and had written to William Wilberforce to petition his help. However, William was disturbed by the way Thom judged other colleagues. He felt this could only harm the cause of the Gospel.

In his letter to the LMS, William wrote,

"Oh, pity we forget the Kingdom of Jesus is not of this world, and any endeavours to unite it with this world cannot but cause discord and a withdrawing of the Spirit's influence."

William also recommended that someone from England with suitable gifts and experience be appointed to serve in Cape Town as the agent of the Society.[126] It was a suggestion that would have far-reaching effects on LMS work in South Africa in the future.

At last William and Johanna were able to leave for Griquatown. William had done all he could to smooth relations with the government while also standing up for the rights of his people at the Orange. The rest was up to God.

During the almost four months they had been in Cape Town, Jansz had been holding the fort in Griquatown. In a letter, he told them that the revival was continuing, though not as powerfully as at first. More people had been baptised and added to the church, and the four men who had been appointed as lay preachers at the Graaff-Reinet conference were zealously engaged in their work. Several people had even told Jansz that they wanted to contribute towards the work of the LMS, and promised gifts including thirty elephant tusks, nine young bulls, four heifers, one ox, twenty-three sheep, and five goats.[127]

Such generosity was a sign of grace, William remarked as he read the news from Jansz. He said to Johanna,

"That is surely evidence of the genuineness of the revival in Griquatown."

Jansz had also reported that he had heard from colleagues working in Namaqualand, far to the west of Griquatown, that many Namaqua as well as Damara people along the coast were listening to the gospel eagerly and responding to it. Even more amazingly, the much-feared brigand, Klass Afrikaner, and his sons, were reportedly wanting to accept the gospel.

"Praise the Lord!" exclaimed William. "I wonder what His Excellency the Governor would say to that?"

He and Johanna were longing to get back. Not all the news Jansz reported was good. Since the Andersons' departure from Griquatown, many people had done little or no gardening, and had instead spent most of their time hunting. The fear of government interference in their lives had also unsettled many. Even more disturbing was news that Jansz himself had not been well. It sounded serious.

Anxious as they were to get back, however, they had to put up with a delay resulting from a disease that hit their cattle. By the end of January, they were still only in the area of the Nieweveld mountains, on the border of the Colony, with a further 500 kilometres to travel.

In the meantime, William had sent two men ahead on horseback to Griquatown. They came back with devastating news:

Jansz was dead.[128]

The men had brought a letter from Christopher Sass, one of the men working in Namaqualand. He had gone to Griquatown to discuss things with Jansz, only to find him dying. The German missionary had been suffering from tuberculosis, a then-unknown illness which many called 'consumption'. According to Sass, Jansz had carried on working and preaching until he could no longer stand or even talk.

On hearing the tragic news, William, Johanna and the others wept.

It was another great blow to the Griqua church.

---

[121] CWM/LMS/05/02/02/019, letter signed by James Read, William Anderson, John Kicherer, Johan Ullbright, Erasmus Smit and William Corner.

[122] Ibid, Anderson to LMS in London, 29 October, 1814

[123] Ibid, Anderson to LMS, 15 November, 1814

[124] Ibid, Anderson to LMS in London, 29 October, 1814

[125] Ibid, Thom to LMS, 16 February, 1814

[126] Ibid, Anderson to LMS, 1 December, 1814.

[127] Ibid, Jansz to Anderson, 2 Dec 1814, Anderson to LMS, from Nieweveld, 24 January, 1815

[128] CWM/LMS/05/02/02/020, Anderson to LMS, 2 February, 1815, from the Nieweveld

CHAPTER 22:

Out of Control

"*Y*ou are a free people. Never allow yourselves to be slaves to the English. The laws made by that Mr Campbell, and enforced by Mr Anderson, are nothing more than rope around your necks. Mr Campbell only came here in order to betray you to the English government in the Cape. He was behind the demand made for your young men to join the Hottentots' Regiment. What evil! They want your young men to fight for them, against your people."

The crowd was hushed as the tall and imposing Coenraad Buys raised and lowered his voice with powerful emotional effect. He was a skilled orator.

"Why do you think Mr Anderson keeps a record of the births and deaths among the people? I'll tell you why. He is an agent of the Cape government and does it only to betray the number of males to your would-be slave masters."[129]

Buys was also a very crafty man. He had little respect for God or religion but he knew many of the people had been influenced by the teaching of the missionaries over many years. He continued in a more gentle, persuasive tone.

"Don't get me wrong. I'm not against the Bible or the gospel, but you should all know that religion is for the soul. The soul has nothing to do with the body and does not affect our customs and habits. You should not let religion curb your freedom and pleasure. Believe me, I know the Bible very well."

Many were swept off their feet by Buys' oratory. He seemed a powerful and successful man. Though a European, he had a large following of Khoikhoi, and several wives in addition to his Dutch wife. They included a Xhosa woman as well as Khoikhoi and Korana women. Later he was to take a Tswana wife as well. He had scores of children.

Buys was also an escapee from Cape justice and was wanted by the Cape authorities for rebellion and insurrection. If anything, it made him more credible to some in the crowd.

Some years previously, Buys had been a leading figure in a revolt by white farmers against the government. He had caused so much trouble in the Colony's eastern border areas that he had been declared an outlaw, and had a price put on his head. He had recently moved north to the Orange where he was safer.

Buys was passionately opposed to the British – and indeed, to all authority in general.[130] His call to throw off the yoke of the English government was now being directed at Griqua rather than Dutch-speaking colonists.

Those who were now eating out of the palm of his hand were a group of dissatisfied former residents of Griquatown.

Ironically, William was seen by some of them as a symbol of the unwelcome authority of the Cape government, just when he was in fact incurring the wrath of the Governor for defending the interests and independence of the Griqua.

So long as association with the mission settlement at Griquatown brought the advantages of free access to trade with the Colony, as well as the much-sought-after gunpowder, most of the Griqua were happy to cooperate with the missionaries and with their traditional chiefs, captains Adam Kok and Berend Berends.

However, once they sensed their freedom was being threatened, and once they felt it was easier and more profitable to trade 'illegally' with farmers in the remote border areas of the Colony, it was different. Why should they have to get a letter or pass from Mr Anderson to enter the Colony to trade, when there were always colonists who would trade with them without such a letter? Why should they have to get gunpowder from 'official' stores in Griquatown, when they could obtain it from unscrupulous farmers?

The uncertainty and violence of this frontier zone, with its clash of competing cultures, unleashed forces that sought to destroy what Griquatown stood for – settled agriculture and a peaceful, ordered society.

The wonderful revival of 1813, which had continued through 1814, seemed to have died with Jansz.

By then the Andersons had been joined by Heinrich (Henry) Helm, a German, and his English wife.[131] The Helms had come to South Africa in 1811 and had been working in Namaqualand. They were a little younger than the Andersons and had two small boys. Four more sons would follow later. The Helms would be even more closely linked to the Andersons' lives in the future.

Meanwhile, they were a great encouragement to William and Johanna, and the two couples enjoyed regular times of prayer together.

They were, however, to face growing difficulties in the work. They found much discussion among church members, but little love and patience. Non-church members seemed even less inclined to listen to them. Gardens were neglected, as were the cattle.

"Mijnheer Anderson," confided the ever-faithful Ian Hendrick, "things seem out of control. No one wants to pay attention to the laws, which we all agreed were good and fair. Some people want to leave Griquatown. They show no respect even for the captains."

"I know," replied William. "I got a mouthful of abuse from one man when I would not condone his forming a commando to attack the Bushmen." The man had wanted to take revenge on the San for allegedly stealing an ox.

"Mijnheer Anderson, they formed a commando anyway," said Hendrick with obvious despair. "I heard they shot four people – a man, two women, and a child."

William was shocked.

"You are right, Mijnheer Anderson," continued Hendrick, "If our people would but look after our cattle better, the Bushmen would not be so tempted to steal. Recently, I went out with captain Kok to look for one of his cows that had strayed off in the night. We saw cattle everywhere, but did not come across a single person looking after them."

There was little that William, his new colleague Henry Helm, or the captains could do to re-establish order. Many distressing things were happening.

On one occasion, after returning from a visit to Hardcastle, William was approached by a Korana who complained about the treatment he and two others had received from a man named Daniels, a resident of Griquatown. Before the case could be investigated, Daniels himself got into a violent argument with his sister. At the height of his temper, he suddenly started coughing blood and, not long after, died.

There appeared to be a general atmosphere of anarchy. William was particularly grieved when Andries Waterboer, one of those appointed in Graaff-Reinet as a lay preacher, was found to have committed adultery.

Over the months, various groups of dissatisfied people left Griquatown. Most of them settled two or three days' journey to the east, at the Harts River. It was to these people that Coenraad Buys made his stirring speeches, and it was in them that he found sympathetic ears.

Then William and Johanna heard even more distressing news.

The 'rebels', who became known as the Hartenaars, were planning to attack Griquatown, take its supply of gunpowder, and kill William, captain Adam Kok, and Piet Pienaar. Berend Berends had heard about these plans when he went hunting in the vicinity of the Harts and had tried to talk to the Hartenaars. William was heart-broken.

"What have I done to earn such hatred and such threats?" he said to Johanna with a deep sigh. "I have laboured among them for sixteen years. Do they not know that all I have sought to do stems from the fact that I love them and desire only the best for them and their families?" Tears filled his eyes.

Johanna too was tearful, but she whispered in William's ear, "My dearest, did not the Saviour say 'No servant is greater than his master. If they persecuted Me, they will persecute you also'?[132] We but follow in His steps."

Captain Kok spoke up.

"Mijnheer Anderson, I can do nothing. I do not know who I can depend on any more. I have known about these threats against you for a long time and wished you were in some safe place far away, for I am powerless to protect you."

By this time, Berends had moved away from Griquatown nearer to Hardcastle with a small group of followers, though he was not at all in sympathy with the rebels.

William and Johanna found it hard to explain to their children why things were so difficult. It was all very unsettling for them. By April 1816, they had welcomed their sixth child, Elizabeth Anna. The Anderson family had also taken in the orphaned son of Jansz, who was named after his father, Lambert.

The Hartenaars had problems of their own.[133] They had many serious conflicts and were living in a pitiful state. They went on cattle raids and got into bloody clashes with the Tswana as well as Korana. Some of the Hartenaars, risking their lives because of the tight control exercised over them by their leaders, escaped from the Harts and returned to Griquatown. They were always welcomed back.

The winter of 1816 was very harsh. and came at the end of a long, hard year for William. He wrote in a letter to the LMS,

"We have had a long night and cold winter. This season has caused me much sorrow of soul. I have been weeping in secret for the day-break. I do think the day is dawning."[134]

One frosty morning, William awoke to snow on the ground.

"Johanna, dear," he whispered to his sleepy wife as he pulled on a warm coat, "shall I have the bell rung this morning? It is so cold, surely no one will come for the early morning prayer meeting."

To his surprise, when the bell rang, more than the usual number of people came. The prayer meeting was a happy, heart-warming hour.

Despite such encouragements, however, it was still far from daybreak for William and for Griquatown.

---

[129] CWM/LMS/05/02/02/020, Anderson to Campbell, 18 January, 1816

130 Sillery, Anthony: The Bechuanaland Protectorate, Cape Town, Oxford University Press, 1952, pp 161-162.

[131] CWM/LMS/05/02/02/021. See also Helm, Charles: The Helm Family History, 1999, pp 7-15.

[132] John 15:20

[133] CWM/LMS/05/02/02/021, Anderson to LMS, 19 April 1816

[134] CWM/LMS/05/02/02/021, Anderson to G Burder, 31 July 1816

CHAPTER 23:

The Way of Forgiveness

*I*t was an impressive sight. Beyond the irrigated gardens, the fields of ripening wheat stretched down the valley for over a mile. The stone church was finished, and Griquatown, despite the problems with the Hartenaars, was a hive of activity.

Old Cornelius Kok, father of captain Adam Kok, had moved with a large following to Griquatown from his settlement further south at Silverfontein in the Kamiesberg mountains. His arrival had improved the attitudes of many of the people, as he had encouraged them to work hard in their fields.[135]

"Mijnheer Anderson," said Old Cornelius, "we need to use force to compel these 'rebels' to submit. They do not even respect the authority of their traditional leaders."

"My honoured friend," replied William as gently as possible, "it is my opinion that forcing obedience would only result in bloodshed. We must avoid this at all cost. I am even prepared to take my family and leave Griquatown if this will help solve the problem."

It was not an easy thing for William to say, for Griquatown was so much a part of his life. Some would have said it was his life.

Old Cornelius, too, knew that force would not be able to change the Hartenaars' minds. He also realised that were the Andersons to leave Griquatown, it might only make things worse for the traditional leaders, who had supported the missionaries.

Apart from Old Cornelius Kok's people, others had made Griquatown their base. They included new LMS recruits who were preparing to settle among the Tswana. To these missionaries' disappointment, their first attempts were frustrated; the Tswana refused to have them.

William wondered if this was the result of the influence of Buys, who had endeared himself to Chief Mothibi by supporting some of his commando raids. Others believed that the Tswana did not want to have the missionaries in their midst because of strong opposition from some of the king's advisors, in particular the medicine men. They feared that allowing any white men to settle among them would bring trouble. They had heard good things about the teachers at Griquatown, but most of what they heard about the white man further south in the Colony was bad.

Things were to change, however, with the coming of James Read from Bethelsdorp.[136]

Read had made a good impression on the Tswana during that first historic trip with John Campbell in July 1813. Although some colleagues found him strong-willed and, at times, domineering, William got on well with him. He felt that Read would be able to win the confidence of the Tswana.

William had also encouraged lay preacher Ian Hendrick, who spoke good Tswana, to consider working among them for a trial period of four years.

"Some may think the Tswana mission is a small matter," William said to Read, "but I feel it is one of the most important that the Society has undertaken. Should that door be opened, there is the potential to reach untold thousands with the good news of the Saviour."

Read nodded. They sat reminiscing as they watched the sun dipping below the barren ridges of the Asbestos Hills, to the west of Griquatown, with its usual splendour.

"James," William continued, "God has blessed us since we came on that ship to Africa back in 1800. We have had our trials, and God knows my present ones are heavy to bear, but the mission to the Tswana encourages me in all my discouragements. The old lion would not roar as he has done, if his kingdom was not getting a shake, more than we are ready to think."[137]

Little did William know that Read was hiding a painful secret. It would shake the LMS and the work of all the missionaries in South Africa.

Before Read left with Robert Hamilton – another pioneer missionary to the Tswana – for Latakkoo, he helped William in the ordination of a member of the Griquatown church. Piet Sabba, who knew the San language very well, wanted to preach to the San and had begun to make a deep impression on those he visited.[138]

"Praise God for his kindness to these poor people," said William in church, after Piet Sabba gave a report to the two hundred-strong congregation one Sunday. "As many of you know," he said with feeling, "the Bushmen have not only been neglected but have also been despised and ill-treated by almost all who have been near them. I trust the time has come when the Lord will show that He has His chosen among them too."

Such an attitude towards the San was not shared or encouraged by the government in the Cape. That very year, 1817, the Governor had forced the closure of two missions to the San – one at Tooversberg, later to be called Colesberg, and the other at Hephzibah on the upper Orange – by recalling the two LMS missionaries involved, Corner and Smit.[139]

Meanwhile, William was being accused by some, including fellow missionaries, of being too soft. They felt he should have taken a stronger line with the Hartenaars and also with those in Griquatown who were blatantly disobeying him and the captains, and had little regard for the 'Campbell rules'.

But William was just being true to himself. Deep down, he longed for peace and reconciliation; he hated confrontation. He did not like having to be policeman as well as pastor in Griquatown, and he was unable to see his way out of the dilemma. As far as he was concerned, he wanted to forgive others, as Christ had forgiven him.

His Christian principles were soon to be tested.

One of the 'rebels' who had caused William more pain than almost any other fell out with other Hartenaars and wished to return to Griquatown. The man was Jacob Kloete.

Kloete's very name gave William bad dreams. He had been found guilty of raping a nine-year-old girl some ten years earlier, and had been one of the most unruly members of the community until the revival of 1813-1814, when he repented, was baptised, and was accepted as a member of the church. When widespread discontent gripped the community and groups of people left for the Harts, however, Kloete was among them. His reversion to his old ways had cut deep into William's sensitive heart.

Now, Kloete wanted to return. Knowing that William and many others in Griquatown would be most reluctant to allow this, he first went to Christopher Sass, who had been in Namaqualand but was now working under William's direction in the newer settlement of Campbell, just over thirty kilometres east of Griquatown.

Kloete asked Sass to write a letter to William, which Sass did, and presented it to the missionary in Griquatown. The letter spoke of how Kloete had begged Sass, with many tears, to intervene on his behalf. As William took the letter from Kloete, he was amazed by his own reactions – he had dreaded the thought of ever meeting Kloete face to face again, but now, he felt neither fear nor anger towards him.

The news that Kloete had returned had meanwhile spread like wild-fire through the community. Curious, nervous people began to gather.[140]

In the school room, William sat with Kloete, and found his heart filling with love for the man as he recounted what had happened since he left Griquatown with the 'rebels'. Every now and again, he broke down and sobbed, unable to control his remorse.

"Mijnheer Anderson, I have been a foolish sinner. I deliberately turned my back on you and on God. Please forgive me, Mijnheer Anderson. I know I have been the biggest hypocrite. I professed to believe and to have turned my back on my old life but somehow, through my own foolish disobedience, I fell again into the clutches of Satan."

William listened without interrupting as Kloete paused to wipe his tear-stained face with both hands.

"Mijnheer Anderson," continued Kloete, "I want to truly repent of this life of sin. If I go on like this, I will only ruin my soul forever and also destroy my wife and my children." Again, he broke down sobbing.

"Please, Mijnheer Anderson, I beg of you to let me return to Griquatown. I will live in peace here and I will try to get the others to come back too. I will return all the cattle I and the others stole from the Tswana when we went raiding with Coenraad Buys."

William looked Kloete in the eyes.

"Jacob," he said warmly, "if you do all that you have said, if you return to the Tswana the cattle you have stolen, and if you sincerely come back in peace, I will receive you."

William knew it was right to forgive. However, as he watched Kloete leave, he had the feeling that not everyone in Griquatown would be so ready to forgive. It was not long before he discovered how right he would be.

Several of the Griqua leaders listened as William related in detail what Kloete had said. They were not impressed, however. Captain Adam Kok was especially cool to the news.[141] Not too many in Griquatown wanted Kloete back.

Soon, rumours were circulating that Kloete had deceived William. The next Sunday, as William came out of church, Kok brought along a San with several nasty wounds on his head. He told William angrily,

"This was done by Kloete. He also stole three oxen belonging to this poor Bushman."

William did not know what to do or think. He could only pray.

The next day, Kok, along with several friends, had a meeting and decided to drive out all those who had returned from the Harts with Kloete. They included Kloete's family. Kloete was not around, however, as he had gone to return the cattle he and others had stolen from the Tswana, as he promised.

"Men, you must not rush," pleaded William. "We must give Kloete time. How do you know he is not truly repentant?"

"Ask the Bushman! Of course he is guilty!" they answered William with unusual roughness.

Kloete returned the following Saturday, and all the charges against him proved to be false. He had done all he said he would, and had even persuaded most of the other Hartenaars to return.

Sadly, although this vindicated William's decision to forgive, not everyone saw it the same way. The Kloete incident alienated the captains, including Berend Berends and Adam Kok, who was especially angry. He threatened to leave Griquatown, but not before going to Latakkoo to talk things over with James Read first.[142]

Unfortunately, Read's involvement was to further complicate things for the Andersons, and Read himself was in deep trouble. His painful secret was soon to become the scandal of the colony.

[135] CWM/LMS/05/02/02/021, Anderson to Campbell, November 1816
[136] Ibid
[137] Ibid
[138] CWM/LMS/05/02/02/022, Anderson to LMS, 15 January 1817
[139] Briggs, Roy and Wing, J, The Harvest and the Hope, United Congregational Church of Southern Africa, Johannesburg, 1970, p 26
[140] CWM/LMS/05/02/02/022, Anderson to LMS 27 April 1817
[141] Ibid
[142] CWM/LMS/05/02/02/022, Read to LMS from Lattakoo, 15 March 1817

James Read

CHAPTER 24:

Adultery

"Good morning, Reverend Thom. On behalf of His Excellency Lord Somerset, the Governor, I must thank you for coming." Christopher Bird, the Secretary to the Governor, shook George Thom's hand and pointed towards several comfortable-looking leather chairs near a log fire in his office. Outside it was cold and windy. "Ah, please take a seat."

"Thank you, Mr Bird," replied Thom. "It seems winter has come early."

"Indeed it does," agreed Bird politely. When Thom was settled in his chair, however, Bird's voice took on a more pompous tone.

"As you may know, Mr Thom, His Excellency and I have just returned from an extensive tour of the eastern border of the Colony," he said.[143] "There are several very urgent matters the Governor wants me to discuss with you."

It sounded ominous. Thom was aware that the government under Lord Somerset was not exactly favourable to missions. In the previous year, two Baptists and two Methodists had been refused permission to do religious work in the Colony. Three of them had left the Cape and gone on to Ceylon or India, while one of the Methodists, a man called Shaw, had stayed back and preached secretly in a hay loft in Cape Town. Only later was he finally given permission to work in Namaqualand.

Thom himself was connected with the more established LMS and acted as the Society's de-facto, though unofficial, representative in Cape Town. Yet even he had only recently been given government permission to remain as the minister of an English-speaking 'non-conformist' church in Cape Town.

The Governor was being influenced, not so much by ministers of the Dutch church, but by the chaplains of the Church of England who were opposed to 'non-conformists'. Thom regarded these 'High Church' men as the greatest enemies of religious liberty in the Colony. On top of all this, the Cape government was at odds with the LMS over a number of issues, including the situations at Bethelsdorp and Griquatown.

Thom knew his interview with the Governor's Secretary might be a confrontational one.

Bird continued, "His Excellency is not prepared to allow any new missionaries to work beyond the borders of the Colony. Those Institutions that do exist, such as the one of Mr Anderson at the Orange, are havens for criminals and runaway slaves, and what's more, even Mr Anderson's converts are not under his control."

Thom was taken aback by both the tone and the virulence of the Secretary's words. Although he tended to sympathise with the government on many issues, Thom felt that the criticism of Anderson and Griquatown was quite unreasonable.[144]

He tried to defend William against these old arguments.

"Mr Bird, sir," he protested, "I fail to see how you can expect a Christian missionary to act as a civil and military servant of government."

Bird coughed with obvious displeasure, and continued as if Thom had not spoken.

"The Governor is of the opinion that the recently published book on the travels of Mr Campbell [145] is scandalous in that it takes the side of Bethelsdorp in agreeing with their criticism of the treatment of the Hottentots and blacks in the Colony."

This was one point on which Thom felt more inclined to concur. Although opposed to slavery, he was nevertheless influenced by the racist attitudes of many white colonists. Living in Cape Town he was also somewhat cut off from the harsh realities facing his missionary colleagues in the inland and border areas.

Bird's next point, however, found Thom in total agreement. It was one of his own hobby horses.

"The Governor wishes to record that it is the view of the Government, that for missionaries to marry Hottentots is a scandal. It is quite unbecoming and lowers the missionary in the eyes of the colonists."

Indeed, there was so much prejudice on this issue that one of the LMS missionaries, Michael Wimmer, could find no one in the Colony to marry him to his sweetheart, Suzanna, a Khoikhoi girl. They eventually gave up waiting and got married 'unofficially' without the approval of either the Dutch or English church. But they could not obtain a marriage certificate from the Landdrost, and it took nearly three years before their marriage was solemnised by the brave Dutch minister in Swellendam.[146]

At the time Thom sat in Bird's office discussing the issue, Wimmer's dilemma was still unresolved. His name was also mentioned by the Secretary as an example of the 'despicable behaviour' of some missionaries.

Then Bird dropped a bombshell.

"Mr Thom, the most serious scandal I have to report concerns one of your most senior men. I believe he is in fact the chief representative of your Society in the Colony." Bird spoke slowly and seemed to relish his words.

"Yes, Mr Thom, the honourable Reverend James Read of Bethelsdorp has taken a young slave girl as a concubine and has gone with her, as well as with his wife, to Latakkoo."[147]

Thom was speechless with shock. This was the first he had heard of such a scandal. After a moment of embarrassing silence, he responded.

"Mr Bird, sir, there must be some grave mistake. It cannot be true, surely?"

"It is common knowledge in the eastern part of the Colony from where, as you know, I and His Excellency have just returned."

Thom was so shocked by this news that, as he left the office of the Governor's Secretary, he had already made up his mind to call a meeting of as many LMS men as he could to discuss the matter. But he would be selective in whom to invite, for they might not only discuss Read, but also a number of other cases, such as that of Wimmer. Some, like Anderson and Helm, were too far away.

"Better not Mr Anderson anyway," thought Thom. "We have differed on this issue of marriage to Khoikhoi women."

William did not exactly encourage cross-cultural marriages, but he was not opposed to them purely on the basis of skin colour. He had in fact felt privileged to officiate at the marriage of his late colleague Jansz, and had told Thom so.

The meeting arranged by Thom took place in Cape Town and lasted an incredible ten days, from 12 to 22 August 1817. Those attending included four new LMS workers who had recently arrived from England, among them Robert Moffat and John Brownlee. Moffat was to become famous for his work with the Tswana in the north, and Brownlee for his work among the Xhosa in the east.

It was a most unsavoury introduction for the young recruits. The meeting was a sad and acrimonious affair. Condemnations were flung left, right and centre, and little attempt was made to show humility or a willingness to forgive.

At times, it was difficult to separate rumour from truth. No one was denying that Read had fallen into the grave error of adultery, nor was anyone trying to condone or excuse his action, but the accusation that he had taken the young woman as a concubine was later proved to be untrue.[148]

The saga had begun three years earlier, not long after the August 1814 missionary gathering in Graaff-Reinet, when Read was back in Bethelsdorp.

What started as a passing attraction to a teenage San girl in his congregation, the daughter of one of his deacons, slowly, over the months, became a secret passion. Read knew it was wrong and tried to put sexual thoughts out of his mind. One day, however, he took physical liberties with the girl. It was only a passing physical touch, but it led to secret meetings that became more and more physical. In the end, Read made the teenager pregnant.

Read was conscience-stricken. He did not know what to do. He knew he was guilty of a blatant sin, yet he felt he had to keep the matter hidden, even from his Khoikhoi wife, Elizabeth Valentyn. Were the affair to be exposed, he knew, he would be seriously discredited in the eyes of the many opponents of his brave though unpopular defence of Khoikhoi rights.

So Read decided that it would be best to move north to help in the mission to the Tswana. There he could have a new start in a new place, and perhaps, his failure would remain a secret.

Before leaving Bethelsdorp, he arranged for the young girl and her parents to return north to their original home near Graaff-Reinet. They left the day before Read and his family themselves departed for Griquatown. The girl was not showing signs of her pregnancy yet, but as he waved them off, the sadness he saw in her eyes brought a lump to his throat. He hoped and prayed the affair would never be discovered.

Read had done what he could to help the girl and her parents, and he had by then also confided in his wife. She had sensed something was wrong but had not confronted her husband. Now, seeing his pain and obvious regret for his actions, she willingly forgave him. She too would keep the whole affair secret.[149]

Some months after Read's departure, however, rumours about the affair began to be whispered in and around Bethelsdorp. Soon, the painful secret Read had been carrying became a much-talked about scandal throughout the Colony and also in England. Missionary James Read had committed adultery and fathered an illegitimate son.

It was only in January 1818, four months after Thom had called the meeting in Cape Town, that copies of the minutes of the meeting reached Griquatown.[150] William and Johanna, along with the Helms, Sass, and the others were shocked. They had seen quite a lot of Read, who was by then working happily, it seemed, with Robert Hamilton and his family among the Tswana in Latakkoo.

William wrote to the LMS in London,

"Oh with what heartfelt sorrow, what deep regret and grief did we read the tale of some of the brethren, particularly of one so eminent and zealous as Brother Read."[151]

He then added,

"Yet for all the evil of this case, let those of us who think we stand, take heed lest we fall."

William knew that Read's affair would do great harm to the missionary cause in the Colony, and seriously undermine their own efforts to help people see the importance of avoiding pre-marital sex and adultery.

But he was also aware that Christians and Christian workers, himself included, were far from immune from the sort of temptation that had overtaken Read. It was a sober reminder of human frailty, rather than an opportunity to feel self-righteous.

William wrote a letter to Read. Warm and brotherly in tone, it encouraged Read to openly confess his sin, if indeed these reports were true, and make things right.[152] William's attitude was one of wanting to forgive, not to condemn or judge.

Read appeared to show genuine repentance. He wrote to several, people, including the directors in London, lamenting his failure and the harm it had done to the work of the Society. He also replied to William's letter. William felt re-assured on reading it.[153]

"I can do no other than treat Read as a brother," he told Johanna. "His having committed adultery is indeed a sad and grievous sin, but he needs our forgiveness and understanding. I just pray the Lord will ever keep me faithful to you, my darling."

William agreed, however, with a resolution adopted at the Cape Town meeting, that Read should not continue to serve as the Superintendent for the work of the LMS in South Africa. George Thom was so scandalised by the whole affair that he eventually resigned from the Society.[154] The directors in London suspended Read from the LMS, though he was accepted back a few years later, after he had made a public confession in the Bethelsdorp church.

Around the same time that Read's affair was exposed, William and the church in Griquatown were encouraged when their own Andries Waterboer, a lay preacher, who had also been accused of adultery, was restored to fellowship in the church after his public confession.[155]

Things, however, were soon to come to a head for the Andersons and their problems in Griquatown. And sadly, James Read was to be a player in the drama.

[143] CWM/LMS/05/02/02/022, Thom to LMS, 29 April 1817

[144] Ibid

[145] Campbell, John: Travels in South Africa, Flagg and Gould, Andover, 1816, Chap VIII, pp 76-97.

[146] CWM/LMS/05/02/02/022, Thom to LMS, 29 April 1817

[147] CWM/LMS/05/02/02/022, Thom to LMS, 29 April 1817

[148] CWM/LMS/05/02/02/024, Folder 1, extracts of missionaries meeting 1817.

[149] Cox, Jeffrey: The British Missionary Enterprise Since 1700, New York, Routledge, 2008, p 109.

[150] CWM/LMS/05/02/02/023, Anderson to LMS, 2 February 1818

[151] Ibid

[152] Ibid

[153] CWM/LMS/05/02/02/023, Anderson to LMS, 7 March 1818

[154] Briggs, Roy and Wing, Joseph: The Harvest and the Hope, UCCSA, Johannesburg, 1970, pp 29,30.

[155] CWM/LMS/05/02/02/023, Anderson to LMS, 2 February 1818

CHAPTER 25:

Good-Bye Griquatown

The return of the Hartenaars had averted open armed conflict, but it did not bring peace to Griquatown. In fact, William's action in forgiving Kloete and welcoming the 'rebels' back, served only to alienate the captains, especially Adam Kok. Their positions as the traditional leaders of the community had been undercut by the 'rebellion' and also, unwittingly, by William.

Though many of the people supported William's decision, Kok and Berends decided to leave Griquatown. Their decision grieved William deeply but he was unable to persuade them otherwise. He had lost their confidence. Kok moved to Campbell, east of Griquatown, joining the bulk of his family who were already there. Berends, with his small following, moved to Danielskuil.

Read, despite the furore over his adultery, continued working with the Hamiltons and Ian Hendrick among the Tswana. Robert Moffat, one of the new recruits, had been refused permission by the Governor to settle north of the Colony, but he was able to make a visit. Earlier, he had bravely gone to Namaqualand and spent time with the notorious brigand Jager Afrikaner, whom he led to faith in Christ.

Just twenty-three years old, Moffat was a man of great talent and strong personality. He was tall and muscular, and had seemingly unlimited energy. However, when he arrived in Griquatown late one evening and knocked on the Andersons' door he was, in his own words, "speechless, haggard, emaciated, and covered with perspiration and dust".[156]

Desperately thirsty, he used sign language to ask William for water. He would later record that "Mr A, expecting such a visitor from the moon, as much as from Namaqualand, was not a little surprised to find who I was . . . Kind-hearted Mrs A instantly prepared a cup of coffee and some food, which I had not tasted for three days".

By the morning Moffat was fully restored, and was ready to join the life of Griquatown. He wrote, "The society of the brethren Anderson and Helm with their partners in labour, was most refreshing to my soul. A crowded and attentive congregation, and the buzz of the daily school, made me forget the toils of the road, and cheerfully did I bear my testimony to the word of grace which had been so blessed among the Griquas."[157]

Moffat was eager to visit the Tswana, and together with William and Johanna and their six children (the latest addition being their fifth daughter, Wilhemina), travelled by ox wagon to Latakkoo.

There they saw a simple, recently-completed church as well as the thatched mud houses of the Reads and the Hamiltons. There was also an irrigation ditch that channelled water five kilometres from the Kuruman river.[158] The visitors enjoyed the opportunity to preach to the Tswana people, and William proudly showed his children to Chief Mothibi.

Through an interpreter, Mothibi told him,

"Five girls, only one son, is not so good. You need more sons."

William smiled. He still had a deep interest in the Tswana, though his work with the Griqua had consumed all his energies.

Mothibi was impressed with Moffat, having heard good reports from some of his people who had met the missionary in Namaqualand. He welcomed him to come and live among the Tswana as their teacher.

It was an invitation Moffat was happy to accept, although he first had to return to the Cape to get permission from the Governor, though he did not tell this to Mothibi.

Later, en-route to Cape Town, Moffat went via Namaqualand and persuaded Jager Afrikaner to accompany him. In Cape Town, the incredulous Governor, Lord Somerset, was so impressed that he gave Afrikaner a full pardon for his many crimes.[159]

The visit to Latakkoo was a refreshing change for William, for he was finding life in Griquatown an increasing strain. While he enjoyed working with his colleague Henry Helm, there was much for the two men and their wives to do.

Up to 300 were attending the various church services on Sunday and official church members numbered almost 200, so there was much need for teaching and counselling. Helm was responsible for the school and was assisted by Waterboer, and they taught the 150 children who attended regularly.

Mrs Helm and Johanna organised various activities for the women, including sewing classes which proved very popular. William and Helm set up a printing press, but only after painstakingly sorting out the pieces of metal type. All the letters had got hopelessly mixed up by the shaking of the wagon on the journey from Cape Town. They were eventually able to print spelling books for themselves and the Tswana mission.[160]

On top of all this work related to the church and the mission, William was responsible for social order in the settlement.

Since the return of the Hartenaars, their problems had appeared to increase. Gardens were neglected, cattle were stolen, and the threat of violence increased, even against William.

There were by then so many guns in the hands of the Griqua and so much gunpowder, that many were far more interested in hunting than in agriculture.

The people could easily sell their ivory and skins in the Colony, and the profits enabled them to buy not only clothes but also more guns, powder, and liquor. As a result, the men neglected their families and were away for long periods of time.

"What concerns me," said William of the young people in Griquatown, "is they do not get much help and encouragement at home. Many parents themselves do not see the need for their children to study."

Helm nodded.

"Of course, many families are really poor and that doesn't help either," he said. "How sad too that so many, even among some of our church members, treat sexual immorality so lightly. The young people are often not given much of an example by their elders."

The government in the Cape still held William responsible for law and order, and expected him to issue passes for anyone wishing to visit the Colony. In 1818, it extended its influence northwards by forming a new sub-magistracy at Beaufort, which was later called Beaufort West. The Landrost of Graaff-Reinet, Andries Stockenstrom, visited Griquatown and, much to William's surprise, made a favourable report to government[161] – even though William had thought that the people were in fact being rather unruly.

It was getting increasingly difficult for William to cope with both the spiritual side of his work and all the other responsibilities that he had on his shoulders. He often talked things over with Johanna.

"My darling, sometimes I see no way out. I cannot seem to get back the cooperation and respect of so many of the people. I feel such a failure. The Lord knows I love the people."

"And they love you too, dear," interrupted Johanna putting her arms around him. "You saw how so many were affected when you suggested to them we might have to leave Griquatown. Since then, so many have come to me begging us not to consider such a thing."

Yet, throughout 1818 and 1819, William and Johanna felt on more than one occasion that the only course open for them would be to leave their beloved Griquatown. They began to wonder if they were the main problem.

Certainly Read had let it be known, more to others than to William, that he thought William was too soft and indecisive. Others, such as Moffat, felt that there should be a clear division between the work of the church and the running of what amounted to an emerging Griqua state. William's problem was that it was all too close to his heart. It was hard for him to stand back and look at the situation objectively.

Finally, late in February 1820, William and Johanna felt the time had come for them to leave. It was a painful decision, but they knew it was right. That Sunday, William preached his last sermon to a solemn congregation.

"Formerly I went out and in among you as your father, your friend, and your guide; but now I am compelled to leave you, viewed by some as nothing better than a dry stalk of maize.[162] Yet, I love you, even those among you who have not always accepted my love or the Saviour's love. You have been my joy and my sorrow, my pleasure and my pain."

William briefly described life when he first came to live among the people, and added,

"We have not laboured in vain. Many have been converted and have turned from darkness to light and from the power of Satan to God."

He then explained why he felt he and Johanna should leave. He had done all he could for the welfare of the people, he said, but as he had lost the support of so many, he felt that God was saying to him that others were now needed to carry on the work. He then asked those in the congregation who had Bibles and could read – and there were by then quite a few – to turn to Jeremiah 17:16.[163] There was a rustling of pages. William read slowly and clearly, but with deep emotion:

"I have not run away from being your shepherd; you know I have not desired the day of despair. What passes my lips is open before you."

There were very few dry eyes as the congregation filed out of church that day.

The news of William's decision to leave spread quickly, even to Campbell and Hardcastle. Many wanted to organise a public meeting to try and persuade the Andersons to stay, but some of the leaders, including Adam Kok, who was still living in Campbell, did not appear to support the idea. It was hard for William, but he knew there were some among the Griqua who were happy to see them go.

What he did not realise was that Read had exacerbated the situation by deliberately undermining his reputation with Kok and some of the other Griqua leaders. He had questioned William's leadership abilities and implied that William was in sympathy with the Cape government, if not actually their agent.

Before saying good-bye and leaving Griquatown for what was to be the last time, William prayed for the people. His final words to them, and prayer for the church among the Griqua, were from Philippians 1:27.

"Whatever happens, conduct yourselves in a manner worthy of the gospel of Christ. Then, whether I come and see you or only hear about you in my absence, I will know that you stand firm in one spirit, contending for the faith of the gospel."

It was a tearful and painful parting for William and Johanna and their family. Johanna held in her arms three-month-old son

Bartholomew Ebenezer, their eighth child. Bartholomew was her father's name, and the name Ebenezer reminded them of the fact that through all the years and despite all their troubles, "Hitherto has the Lord helped us". Little B.E., as they called him, was to remind them of God's faithfulness.

The Helms and about 200 Griquatown residents, mostly church members, waved them off as they and their small party headed south for the Orange river.

---

[156] Moffat, Robert: Missionary Labours and Scenes in Southern Africa, London, 1842, Chapter XI, pp 165,6.

[157] Ibid

[158] CWM/LMS/05/02/02/024, Anderson to LMS, 22 February 1819; & Moffat reporting on same visit in October 1818

[159] Moffat: Missionary Labours and Scenes, Chapter XI, pp 178-80.

[160] CWM/LMS/05/02/02/023, Helm to LMS, 7 March 1818

[161] Cape Town Archives, 1 G/R 16/7, no. 1016; and mentioned in Schoeman, Karel: The Mission at Griquatown 1801-1821, Griquatown, 1997, pp 18, 20, 96; & CWM/LMS/05/02/02/024, Anderson 22 February 1819

[162] Moffat, Robert: Missionary Labours and Scenes in Southern Africa, 1842, p 198.

[163] CWM/LMS/05/02/02/025, Anderson to Burder, 24 August 1820

Dr John Philip

CHAPTER 26:

New Directions

*I*t was Saturday evening and the last rays of the setting sun were giving way to the brilliant stars of the Milky Way. It had been a hot day. Robert Moffat and his young bride Mary were enjoying the cool of the evening air when two wagons approached. Moffat strained to see who was sitting up front with the driver of the leading wagon.

"Would you believe it! Brother Anderson, what are you doing here?" Moffat could hardly believe his eyes. William jumped down and his men prepared to outspan the oxen.

"Robert, I could well ask you the same question," responded an equally-surprised William. They were just south of the Orange River, which the Anderson party had just crossed earlier in the day.

Just then, another familiar face joined the circle. It was John Campbell, the LMS director who had visited the Tswana with William. He was on his second visit from England.[164]

"Brother Anderson, what a surprise! We are on our way to visit you and now here you are meeting us," he said.

"We have been expecting your visit for some time, Brother Campbell," said William overjoyed to see his colleagues. "I've been eager to see you again, and was also looking forward to meeting Dr Philip. I had given up hope of seeing you in Griquatown but fully expected I'd see you in Cape Town."

Campbell and Dr John Philip, the new LMS Superintendent, had arrived in Cape Town almost a year earlier. They had been sent by the Society to try and calm the situation in the wake of the various scandals in South Africa.[165] The two men had visited Bethelsdorp and other places, and Campbell was now heading north. Dr Philip was still in Cape Town.

Had the circumstances of their surprise meeting that evening been happier, they might have had a big celebration. Instead, they soon found themselves listening to William's sad explanation of why he had felt led to leave Griquatown.

They exchanged letters. William had reports and letters for Campbell, as well as letters for Campbell from others, including Read. There were letters for the Andersons too, including some from England. Though weary from the day's travelling, everyone retired to read their mail by candle-light. They would meet for more prayer and discussion the next morning.

Campbell showed Moffat the letter he received from Read. In it, Read blamed William for all the troubles in Griquatown. He said he had been in regular contact with the Griqua captains and had advised them that for there to be proper social order, and for the captains to regain their proper authority, William would have to go.[166]

"Mr Campbell, you simply have to show this to Brother Anderson," said Moffat adamantly. "He clearly has no idea that Read has been so much behind his problems."

"I don't think it will help to show him," replied Campbell hesitantly.

The two men had slightly differing views of William. Campbell's view was that William was 'a nervous, timid man, fond of temporal power and yet not willing to do anything to discipline the people'. But Moffat disagreed. He had been very impressed with William during his earlier visit to Griquatown and Latakkoo, and strongly defended him. He had not, however, been impressed with Read and had serious doubts about his motives.

Now, with Read's letter before them, Campbell found it hard to argue with Moffat.

"I have to confess, it looks as if Read has been a deceiver," he admitted.

"It is blatantly obvious," retorted Moffat. "Anderson must see this. It is only right that he has the fuller picture. The Griqua have been his life."

Campbell reluctantly agreed.

The next day, he handed Read's letter to William, briefly explaining why he and Moffat thought he should see it.

"It is a little disturbing, William, but we think you should see it anyway," he said, somewhat tentatively.

William went to read it in his tent, which had been pitched next to that of the Moffats. Moffat did not mean to eavesdrop, but he could hear exclamations of amazement as William read the letter.[167]

"I am hurt. I am hurt," a distressed William could be heard saying. Moffat then heard what he thought were quiet sobs.

Johanna was with William. He showed her Read's letter, and after reading it, they both knelt together in prayer.

The following morning as the Andersons were getting ready to leave, Moffat hastily wrote a letter for them to take to Dr Philip expressing his warm support for the Andersons.[168] He felt they had been saintly in the way they handled their disappointments.

William, meanwhile, found himself struggling, like never before, with strong feelings of self pity, anger and bitterness. He had been astonished at Read's treachery and deceitfulness.

Even after having arrived in Cape Town weeks later, he received letters from Read that were polite and full of flattery.

He knew that at the same time Read was saying the most critical and negative things about him to Campbell.

Over the following months, despite the support and understanding of so many, including Dr Philip,[169] William fought a battle within himself. His whole life's work seemed to be in ruins. He had been prepared to give his life for the people and had wished to spend the rest of his days with them, but now he was virtually cut off from those he had loved and served for so long. Now that he was fifty, with his best years behind him, he wondered whether he could pick his life up again. It was a devastating experience.

As he mulled over what had happened, he found negative, critical, even hateful thoughts beginning to overwhelm him. At times, he was tempted to give up. He felt like a miserable failure.

All this time he was supported by Johanna, who could feel his pain and sense his turmoil. It was his regular study of the Bible and prayer, however, that kept him from despair. He spent time studying the lives of people in the Bible who had suffered far more than he. The examples of Jeremiah and some of the other prophets were particularly encouraging, as was that of the Apostle Paul. Paul's letters to the Galatians and Corinthians became very precious to William. Most of all, he was moved by the example of the Saviour who humbled Himself, even to the extent of allowing Himself to be rejected and nailed to a cross by the very ones He had come to save.[170]

William had a clear conscience about all he had done in Griquatown. He knew he had made mistakes and was far from perfect, but he also knew his motives had been right and he had sought to do everything as well as he could. He knew that he could be proud and stubborn at times, but he had always sought to glorify God and build God's Kingdom, and not his own.

He began to see that God was sovereign even in his circumstances. Maybe He had allowed people like Read to do what he had done. Maybe He had another plan for him and his family. Maybe He had wanted them to leave Griquatown so as to lead them into a new work.

William began to experience healing for his hurt. He sensed the Holy Spirit renewing his spirit and giving him new joy and freedom.

Throughout this period, the Andersons were living at an LMS station called The Caledon Institute at Zuurbraak, near the town of Swellendam. It was a beautiful spot right up against the Langeberg ('Long Mountains'), one of the ranges in the southern Cape mountains. Their sturdy stone house faced those mountains, which were covered with beautiful forests. The land was well-watered and fruitful. It was a very different environment from the barren hinterland with which he and Johanna were so familiar.

Zuurbraak was not without its difficulties, though. Dr Philip hoped William could sort out some of the problems which stemmed from Johanna's brother-in-law, Johannes Seidenfaden.[171] After working under tough conditions in arid Namaqualand, Seidenfaden and Maria had moved to Zuurbraak, but there Seidenfaden turned out to be a disaster. The LMS had to dismiss him following problems over drink and neglect of duty.[172] He also got into a dispute with the government over land rights. Lord Somerset had declared that the land belonged to the remnants of the Khoikhoi tribe living at Zuurbraak, and could not be appropriated by whites, Seidenfaden included.[173]

William threw himself into the work at Zuurbraak and soon, the local people were speaking highly of their new missionary. William felt at home, for the people were similar to his beloved Griqua, certainly in looks. He also enjoyed preaching at the farms of white colonists in the neighbourhood, and always received a warm welcome and generous hospitality from the farmers and their workers.

While the Andersons did their best in the short time they were in Zuurbraak, it would be some years before The Caledon Institute would be back up on its feet again. Their colleagues in Griquatown, Henry and Charlotte Helm, would see Zuurbraak prosper.[174] Little would they know that the two families would be inextricably linked: Many years later, their daughter Johanna would live and work at Zuurbraak as the wife of one of the Helm boys.

Towards the end of 1821, Dr Philip visited the Andersons in Zuurbraak on his return from a tour of the LMS stations in the east of the Colony.[175]

"William," he said as they sat on the porch of the simple mission house, "I have a proposal for you."

Dr Philip was a godly man with great intellect. Before the LMS asked him to head its work in South Africa, he had been a well-known pastor in Aberdeen, Scotland. In the two-and-a-half years since his arrival in the Cape in February 1819, he had made a favourable impression on the Governor and had also impressed the recently-arrived English settlers in the eastern Cape – the so-called 1820 Settlers. Later, however, both the government and the settlers would change their minds about Dr Philip because of his brave and out-spoken support of Khoikhoi and black rights.

Dr Philip and William got on well from the very beginning. William respected Dr Philip and greatly valued his advice and leadership.

"I'm all ears, Dr Philip," said William.

"What would you and Johanna think about the idea of moving further east to Pacaltsdorp to assist Johann Messer? It is a most strategic place and I feel it has great potential. As you may know, there was a true work of God done there by the late Mr Pacalt. It is a story all right! But now the work needs someone with your experience and gifts. Mr Messer has a few problems. I believe you may be the right person for Pacaltsdorp."

Was this God's new direction for William and Johanna?

---

[164] Campbell, Travels, II, pp 53-58

[165] Briggs, Roy and Wing, Joseph: The Harvest and the Hope, UCCSA, Johannesburg, 1970, p 30; and le Cordeur, Basil: The Occupations of the Cape, 1795-1854 in An Illustrated History of South Africa, Jonathan Ball Publishers, Johannesburg, 1986, p 86.

[166] CWM/LMS/05/02/02/025, Moffat at Orange River to Dr Philip in Cape Town, 6 March 1820

[167] Ibid

[168] Ibid

[169] CWM/LMS/05/02/02/025, Philip to LMS, 3 June 1820

[170] CWM/LMS/05/02/02/025, Anderson in Zwellendam to Burder in London, 24 August 1820

[171] Ibid

[172] Briggs, Roy & Wing, Joseph: The Harvest and the Hope, UCCSA, Johannesburg, 1970, p 20, 41; and Philip, John: Researches in South Africa, Vol I, p 284.

[173] Philip, Researches, Vol I, p 292.

[174] Tomlinson, L.: Geskiedkundige Swellendam, 1945

[175] CWM/LMS/05/02/02/028, Anderson to Burder, 25 January 1822

CHAPTER 27:

Pacaltsdorp

*T*he Outeniqua Mountains were beautiful, sometimes shrouded in mist, sometimes shades of mauve and purple contrasting with the bright blue of a cloudless sky. Between its ramparts and the crashing breakers of the wild and enchanting coastline lay the gently rolling hills of the narrow coastal plain. Across the coastal plain itself, tumbling rivers had over the centuries, gouged out deep, ravine-like valleys as they wound their way from the mountains to the sea.

The Khoikhoi settlement of Pacaltsdorp lay close to the sea, but had a good view of the mountains to the north. Once called Sandy Hill before being renamed Hoogte Kraal ('High Village'), it was one of the last remaining villages of the once numerous 'Outeniqua' people, the original Khoikhoi inhabitants of this fertile and forested land.

White settlers had begun moving into Outeniqualand in the eighteenth century. By 1811, when the Governor Lord Caledon proclaimed the area the District of George and the town was laid out, there were already many white farmers in the area. Both district and town were named after King George III of England.

The Outeniqua Khoikhoi had, by then, been deprived of much of the land over which they had traditionally roamed while herding their cattle. Their tribal structures, traditions and culture had largely been lost and they were looked down upon by the white colonists, who saw them as 'lazy' and 'uncivilized', and in some cases, treated them cruelly.

It was thus to a degraded and broken people, demoralised by drink, and a by-word for thieving, that the first LMS missionary to the Outeniqua Khoikhoi, Carl Pacalt, came in 1813. He arrived after Dit Kop, captain of the Outeniqua, having heard of the work done at Bethelsdorp, pleaded for a missionary to be sent to help his people.[176] William had met Pacalt when the latter first arrived at the Cape in 1810.

As Pacalt lived and worked with the people, like William had done among the Korana and Griqua at the Orange River, the gospel began to bring remarkable changes among the people. Tragically, he died after only five years of work, and Hoogte Kraal was renamed Pacaltsdorp in his honour.[177] Johann Messer had come to replace Pacalt, and had been there only two years when the Andersons arrived.

It was their practice each evening to have family prayers with their children, and the first night in Pacaltsdorp was to be no exception. Surrounded by their half-unpacked boxes of belongings, William and Johanna prayed together with their children,

"Oh Lord, please use us to carry on the work others have begun and please use us at Pacaltsdorp to build Your Kingdom for Your glory. Amen."

It did not take long for them to settle in.

Realising that there was a great need for teaching, William focused his energies on preaching as well as organising the school. He also knew that he needed to 'live out' what he taught, so that he and his family might be an example.

When the Andersons arrived, ninety-two of the 300 people living at Pacaltsdorp were members of the church. As the number of people attending the Sunday services grew, plans to build a large stone church were soon afoot.

As he threw himself into his work, William was unaware that the Governor, Lord Somerset, had got a little upset over the manner of his appointment to Pacaltsdorp. The Governor's Secretary Christopher Bird, wrote to Dr Philip noting William's arrival.

"Sir, the Magistrate of the George district has reported to His Excellency the Governor, the arrival at the Hoogte Kraal of Mr Anderson, late a missionary among the Griqua, and His Excellency has desired me in consequence to point out to you that when you may wish to place missionaries at any places within this colony His Excellency expects that his consent to the measure shall be previously obtained. It is no personal objection to Mr Anderson which has induced His Excellency to make this remark, far less a disinclination to support the views of the London Missionary Society, but it will be obvious to you that it is His Excellency's duty to watch over cases of this nature."[178]

Dr Philip sent the Governor a polite but firm reply, referring to the settlement as Pacaltsdorp – not Hoogte Kraal – and asking for clarification as to whether missionaries were now to be appointed by the government or, as he had hitherto presumed, by the LMS. He asked who would be responsible for removing them if such a measure were necessary, and added,

"Pacaltsdorp is in great need of more help and Mr Anderson is the most suitable and experienced person available."

Dr Philip also said there were plans at Pacaltsdorp to build more houses and a 'neat church', as well as to set up a blacksmith shop and a carpenter shop.[179]

Soon, the government began to get good reports of what was happening at Pacaltsdorp. In December 1823, it sent a high-level delegation, His Majesty's Commissioners of Inquiry[180], to Pacaltsdorp. Accompanying the visitors were Dr Philip, the Landdrost of George District and other local dignitaries. At the

Sunday service, William preached as usual, and was pleased to discover that the members of the delegation were impressed.

"Wonderful singing, Mr Anderson," said the Landdrost to William after the service. "The Commissioners have been very impressed with the children."

"Indeed, Mr Anderson," chipped in one of the Commissioners, Major Colebrooke. "They all looked so smart in their pretty clothes, and I couldn't get over the way they read from the Scriptures with such fluency and such liveliness."

William smiled proudly.

"They are a delight, I must admit, and they do sing and read beautifully," he said. "We have friends in England to thank for their smart clothes."

Johanna nodded. "Yes, though second-hand, the clothes are much appreciated by the children and their families."

Sunday, 19 June 1825, was a special day for Pacaltsdorp.

"What a beautiful building!"

"It is magnificent!"

Visitors had come from far and near for the official opening of the great stone church, and stood outside admiring the masonry work and the massive Norman-style tower. Inside, the pews, balcony, and platform, with a large pulpit in the centre, were all made of local timber. It had been, for its day, an ambitious project, but had taken only eighteen months to complete.[181]

The church was packed with over five hundred, and many more were standing outside.[182] The men were seated on the right side of the church, the women on the left. The atmosphere was electric with excitement.

During the service, before Dr Philip rose to speak, William found his thoughts going back for a moment to the large reed and mud church that he had built among the Griqua. Now, as he looked over the congregation in Pacaltsdorp, he was deeply moved by what he saw. He shared his thoughts with Dr Philip after the service.

"As I listened to the people sing, and as I saw them sitting in the House of God, many with Bibles in their hands, I was filled with a sense of wonder at what God has done. These same people, but a few years ago, were in abject poverty and moral degradation, wandering about naked except for a piece of sheep skin, without any knowledge of the Saviour."

"It is a wonderful testimony to what God has done," agreed Dr Philip.

"Sadly, though, it has to be said," continued William, "that many colonists, despite the evidence before them, are too prejudiced to admit that missionary work is worthwhile, nor do they offer any assistance."

Nevertheless, William and the people of Pacaltsdorp did find increasing recognition from local colonists and officials. Several farmers began attending the main Sunday service with their families, showing little if any prejudice.

Every Sunday was a busy day for the Andersons.

It began, as always, with an early morning prayer meeting, followed by an adult instruction class, then the main worship service, then a singing service. The people of Pacaltsdorp, like those in Griquatown during the revival, loved to sing. In the afternoon, another worship service was held, followed by an adult class and a testimony meeting. In the evening, William held a catechism class for adults and one for children. He was assisted by Roger Edwards, an artisan missionary who had been very involved in the building of the new church.[183]

One evening, after the catechism class, a young man came up to William. "Mr Anderson, I am surprised at the change in me," he said.

"Oh yes, Piet," replied William, "in what way?"

"Well, Mr Anderson, I find I have more assurance of what I believe. Now I know what is right and wrong. I am much happier."

Piet was not the only one to have this experience. William was delighted to see so many, both adults and children, growing in their knowledge of the Scriptures. Many who previously depended upon their feelings and were fond of telling about their dreams, were finding comfort and guidance in the Bible.[184] It was transforming their behaviour and their inter-personal relationships.

As a result, the people of Pacaltsdorp began to get a reputation for honesty and good work. A colonist living in Mossel Bay further along the coast had the highest praise for a carpenter he hired from Pacaltsdorp. Others told William that they preferred Pacaltsdorp men as wagon drivers for long trips, because they were more reliable than others.[185]

Johanna, meanwhile, had her hands full with a large and active family. There were four young teenagers, a ten-year-old, a nine-year-old, and the youngest, Bartholomew, now seven.

The older children had begun to assist their parents in the church and in the day school. Maria was only fifteen and Kitty fourteen, but they had already started a school for needlework and knitting. Johannes, their eldest, was helping in the catechism class.[186]

William and Johanna often worried about their children's own education. They did all they could to teach them themselves, and were delighted when friends in England sent them books for the children. Their colleague, Edwards, also tutored Johannes.

The Andersons had also taken in a local boy, Boezak Platjes. He reminded them a little of Lambert Jansz's orphan, whom they had had to leave – with much reluctance – with his grandfather, Piet Pienaar, in Griquatown. The children often asked their parents about little Lambert. All of them wondered. Many years later, Lambert would become an advisor to Griqua leader Nicholas Waterboer, the son of Andries Waterboer.

Johanna's heart still hurt whenever she remembered the loss of their eldest son, William Bartholomew, way back in 1810 in Cape Town. She also grieved over their more recent loss of George Peterus, who had been born soon after their arrival in Pacaltsdorp. He had died less than three months after his birth. Despite having such a large and active family, the death of little George had been very painful for William and Johanna.

Though life in Pacaltsdorp was happy and full, William and Johanna longed for news of Griquatown for which they prayed frequently. The occasional letter or report they received left many of their questions unanswered.

"You know Johanna, I often wonder how our beloved friends are doing in Griquatown," said William as they made their way to the church for the afternoon service one Sunday. "I sometimes find myself just longing to see them again."

As William came out of the great stone church after the service that day, 8 October 1826, he could hardly believe his eyes.

[176] Campbell, Travels, Chap V, pp 58. 60-62.

[177] Briggs, Roy & Wing, Joseph: The Harvest and the Hope, UCCSA, Johannesburg, 1970, p 21

[178] CWM/LMS/05/02/02/028, C Bird to Philip, 20 February 1822

[179] CWM/LMS/05/02/02/028, Philip to Bird, various correspondence, March & April 1822

[180] CWM/LMS/05/02/02/029, Report for Pacaltsdorp, 1823

[181] Anderson, T.A.: The Story of Pacaltsdorp, 1957, Chapter VI, pp 30-33.

[182] CWM/LMS/05/02/02/031, Anderson to Burder, 18 August 1825

[183] Ibid; and also Anderson, T: The Story of Pacaltsdorp, 1957, Chapter VI, p 34.

[184] CWM/LMS/05/02/02/030, Report for Pacaltsdorp, 1824

[185] CWM/LMS/05/02/02/032, Anderson to LMS, 16 January 1826

[186] Ibid

CHAPTER 28:

News From Afar

illiam blinked and rubbed his eyes in disbelief. Several men, all Griqua, were dismounting from their horses. Not far behind them were three ox-drawn wagons, and more Griqua. The travel-weary party had just arrived in Pacaltsdorp.[187]

Seeing William, the Griqua visitors gave a spontaneous shout. William leapt down the steps of the church, almost tripping, and ran towards them. Johanna and the children were not far behind. One by one William embraced the men, and bowed politely as he shook hands with the women. He was so excited he could hardly speak. Both he and many of the Griqua were wiping back tears of joy. William longed to hug the little children but some of them, having not seen him before, clung to their mothers' skirts shyly.

A large crowd watched this emotional reunion in amazement. The display of affection between the Andersons and their Griqua visitors surprised some, especially whites from the village of George who had been at the afternoon worship service.[188]

The visitors had brought some of the Andersons' belongings from Griquatown, including a few cattle and sheep, but their main purpose in coming had been simply to visit their old friend and pastor.[189] The journey had taken over two months, and involved the crossing of several mountain passes, including the dangerous Cradock Pass in the Outeniqua Mountains.

The visitors, who also included a few Korana and Tswana, stayed for almost three weeks, giving the Andersons time to catch up on news about Griquatown and the other settlements north of the Orange River.

"How is my dear friend Andries Waterboer?" asked William. "I hear he was made captain."

"Yes, Mijnheer Anderson, that was nearly six years ago. He is well respected and liked by the people."

"Is he still active in the church?"

"Oh yes, he has always supported the missionaries in their work."

"Tell me about my friend, captain Adam Kok," continued William. "I heard he passed away a couple of years ago, only a year after his dear father, old Cornelius Kok. Was he ill for some time? How is his family? Are they still living at Campbell?"

William and Johanna spent many long and happy hours with their Griqua friends. They had heard that the situation among the Griqua had been far from settled, but it was good to get first-hand information.

The problems with which they had grappled before their sad departure appeared to have been even deeper than William had realised. Despite what James Read had told the captains, the departure of the Andersons had not changed things for the better.

Like William, Henry Helm, along with Christopher Sass in Campbell, had been accused of being government spies. A government agent, John Melvill, had been sent to handle such things as the issuing of passes to the colony and anything to do with the Cape government, and his arrival had brought much relief to the missionaries.

Melvill was a warm supporter of the LMS and admired the missionaries for all they were doing, but he too found his work fraught with difficulties.[190] He would leave later, feeling he had not accomplished much. Still, his role in bringing a much clearer separation between 'church and state', as Robert Moffat had urged, had been crucial.

Andries Waterboer, meanwhile, had established himself as a credible and good leader, though he, too, faced the same social problems that had been plaguing the community just before the Andersons left.

The visitors from Griquatown kept William and his family on the edge of their seats as they described a terrible battle between a Griqua commando led by Waterboer and a marauding Sotho-speaking tribe, the Tlokwa, referred to as the Mantatee. They were so named after their powerful Chieftainess or Queen, Mantatisi.

Although the battle had taken place some three years earlier, and the Andersons had read about it in news from the LMS[191], they were shocked to hear all the graphic details.

A Mantatee force of several thousand men, having recently overrun the Rolong, had threatened to attack Chief Mothibi and the Tlhaping at Kuruman. Mothibi sent Waterboer an urgent appeal for help, and the Griqua, using the superior power of their 'thunder and lightning' – their guns – routed the huge Mantatee army with the loss of only one man. The Mantatee lost over 400 dead.

"I was there," said Jan Willem, the man relating the incident to the Andersons. "Mr Melvill and Rev Moffat was also there."

William gulped.

"Were they not some distance away, Jan?" he asked.

"No, they was in the middle of the battle. Spears and knobkerries is flying everywhere, there is smoke from huts which the Mantatee did set on fire, our guns is firing, blood and noise is all around." Willem's grammar was not perfect, but his description of the battle was vivid.

"What were Mr Melvill and Mr Moffat doing?" asked William with deep concern. "Were they not injured?"

"They was trying to help the wounded and dying, especially the women and children," replied Jan.

"How come there were women and children on the battlefield?" Johanna asked.

"The Mantatee deliberately put their women and children in front of them," said Jan.

"As human shields!" exclaimed William. He looked at Johanna and they both shuddered.

Willem nodded. "Those wounded is sometimes killed by their own people. I see myself. In the end, they is all turn around and run. They just running and leaving everything, including their cattle. There is dead bodies, spears, shields and other things lying all over the place."

"How terrible," said William. "I'm glad we were spared such madness when we were there."

"Yes, Mijnheer Anderson, we remember," said another man. "Some of us used to call you 'the peace-maker'. You spoke of using the weapons of peace and love and never wanted us to use force to sort out disputes."

On the third day of the visit of his Griqua friends to Pacaltsdorp, William noticed that one of the men, a Korana, was very depressed. William asked him what was troubling him, and the story came out.

Just before descending the Cradock Pass on the northern side of the mountains, the party from Griquatown had been given some liquor by a white farmer called Kleu. Without the knowledge of the leader of the group, Kleu had tried to barter with one of the Korana. He wanted to exchange a horse, four sheep, a goat, and some other articles for a little San boy who was with the Korana. The Korana obliged. When the leader of the party heard what had happened, he was very angry, but was too afraid to confront the farmer over the matter.

William asked his colleague Edwards to go over the pass, find Kleu and try to get him to release the San boy. He succeeded in finding Kleu, but the farmer was in no mood to listen and gave Edwards a mouthful of insults, even threatening violence if he did not get off his property immediately.

Undeterred, William reported the affair to the Landdrost in George and asked for his help. The Landdrost ordered that Kleu return the boy, and the Korana return what he had received from Kleu. This, despite what Kleu had originally promised, happened to be only four sheep, one goat, and a knife. William agreed to pay for one of the sheep, which had in the meantime got lost.[192]

Three weeks passed by very quickly. Reluctant and tearful farewells were exchanged when the party from Griquatown finally left Pacaltsdorp. William accompanied them on horseback as far as the Cradock Pass. He knew he might never see them again.

Four years later, in 1830, Robert Moffat and his wife visited Pacaltsdorp. With them was nine-year-old daughter Mary, who was born in Griquatown and who was yet to meet her future husband David Livingstone, the famous explorer missionary.

Moffat told William more about the gruesome battle between the Mantatee and the Griqua in which he and Melvill had been caught.

He, his wife and Robert Hamilton had been in Kuruman when the settlement came under threat from the Mantatee, who had themselves been driven south by the Matabele.

"These are far fiercer fighters, I can tell you!" said Moffat of the Matabele. "Both John Melvill and I, along with Waterboer and his men, tried all we could to persuade the Mantatee to make peace with Mothibi and not attack Kuruman, but all to no avail. The Mantatee suddenly, without any warning whatsoever, attacked the Tlhaping."

"The Griqua victory," Moffat added, "saved Mothibi and his people from an even worse slaughter than that which befell the Mantatee."[193]

Southern Africa was a cauldron of clashing cultures and languages. It was a time of savage violence, sparked by rampaging Zulu armies from Natal and unleashed in various part of the sub-continent. This violent movement – the Mfecane – brought death, destruction, and starvation to many tribes in southern Africa, including the Sotho and the Tswana.

"It is so sad to hear of all the violence and senseless killing among the black nations, whom one would think have so much in common," said William.

"Of course I agree with you," said Moffat thoughtfully, "but is it not the history of mankind? Just look at our European wars!"

William nodded in agreement.

"Whether it be in Europe or Africa – when will violence give way to love?" he wondered.

But William knew the answer to his own question. It could happen only when nations, and individuals within those nations, came to know and experience God's love.

---

[187] CWM/LMS/05/02/02/032, Report for Pacaltsdorp, Anderson 1 November 1826
[188] Ibid
[189] Anderson, T.A.: The Story of Pacaltsdorp and Some Reminiscences, George, 1957, p 29.
[190] CWM/LMS/05/02/02/026, Philip to LMS, 30 August 1820; & CWM/LMS/05/02/02/030, Melvill to LMS, May 1824
[191] CWM/LMS/05/02/02/029, Moffat to LMS, 23 July 1823
[192] CWM/LMS/05/02/02/032, Anderson, 1 November 1826
[193] Robert Moffat in Missionary Labours and Scenes, Chap XXII, pp 354-372.

CHAPTER 29:

Fighting For Fairness

*W*illiam was a pastor. Committed as he was to helping people in practical ways, he was also prepared to stand up for what was right and fair, even when it was costly to do so. Sometimes this got him into trouble, made him unpopular, or made him some enemies. Though he was not a campaigner in the political arena like LMS Superintendent Dr John Philip, William felt it was his duty to stand up for the rights of the under-privileged in society.

He and Dr Philip, for example, were in agreement regarding the treatment of the Khoikhoi. When Dr Philip visited Pacaltsdorp, the two men discussed the subject at length.

"Quite apart from the written law," said Dr Philip as he sat relaxing in the Anderson home after a delicious evening meal prepared by Johanna, "there are certain rights which human beings possess, and of which they should not be deprived. To so deprive them would be blatant injustice. Such rights include the right to a fair price for one's labour; exemption from cruelty and oppression; the right to choose where you live, and to enjoy the company of one's wife and children. To deprive our Hottentots of these rights is to violate the laws of nature and civilized nations."[194]

"I agree, John," replied William. "You have a wonderful way with words, and you are absolutely right! If only those with influence in government would listen to your ideas, society as we know it could be very different."

Dr Philip's opinions would indeed be heard by influential people both in the Cape and in Britain. When he published his two-volume work, Researches in South Africa, in 1828, he strongly attacked many of the discriminatory regulations against the Khoikhoi. But he was way ahead of his time in the discussion of human rights and justice, and caused a storm in the Colony.

William, too, fought his own battles for fairness in Pacaltsdorp. One such battle had to do with alcohol, a social issue that entangled him for several months, and involved extensive correspondence and lengthy argument. He called it the Stietz affair.[195]

For some time William had noticed that some of the people living in Pacaltsdorp were having problems with liquor. He warned them from the pulpit and also when he visited them in their homes.

"You must not enslave yourselves to this evil," he told a group of young men. "In one minute flat you drink the stuff, and then for months you will be trying to pay off your debt in timber or by hard labour."

"No, Mr Anderson," protested one of the boys, "Mr Stietz lets us buy on credit and we just pay him back later."

"That's just it, Piet," said William, "You still have to pay back and no doubt with interest on top."

Stietz was the Pachter (licensed retailer) of George. He had a monopoly on the sale of alcoholic beverages, and had a flourishing 'canteen', or store, that sold mostly liquor.

Looking into the matter, William discovered that Stietz was deliberately selling liquor and other commodities on credit to local Khoikhoi, including some residents of Pacaltsdorp, and charging very heavy interest. As a result, many got hopelessly into debt and had to contract themselves to work for Stietz. In writing up these contracts, Stietz paid little attention to proper legal procedures.

Things came to a head when several men from Pacaltsdorp were involved in a big argument with Stietz. The Pachter had the men savagely beaten and thrown into prison, but when William went to see Stietz, he was not interested in talking.

In desperation, William went to the Landdrost of George, van der Riet.

Explaining the situation to the Landdrost, he gave details of those who had run up huge debts, and pointed out that several contracts drawn up by Stietz seemed to be illegal. Some of those in debt, he pointed out, had been beaten or illegally imprisoned. Even children had been sold or offered drink on credit.

"Whole families are being destroyed by this man's greed," said William. "Something must be done to curb his immoral behaviour, especially his using such illegal methods to enslave people to himself as contracted labourers."

"Reverend Anderson, I am satisfied you have a serious case against the Pachter, Mr Stietz," said the Landdrost, "but I too have found him extremely difficult to handle. He has a lot of influence and is a very strong character."

"Do you think we will have to take this matter to a higher authority then?" asked William.

"It does unfortunately seem to be necessary," replied van der Riet. "I suggest you present your case in a memorandum to His Excellency the Governor. I will let it be known that I support you in this action."

Over the next few months, an exchange of correspondence took place between William and the LMS representative in Cape Town, Richard Miles and also between Miles and the Governor.[196] At the time, Dr Philip was away in England and Miles was acting as his deputy.

Finally, on 1 August 1827, the Colonial Secretary, Sir Richard Plasket, wrote to Miles and to the Landdrost of George on behalf of the Acting Governor, General Richard Bourke.

Stietz's actions, he said, broke the laws regarding contracts and treatment of the Hottentots.[197] Stietz, therefore, was to be informed he would no longer be in government employment, and that all Pacaltsdorp residents under contract to him were to be released from their contracts immediately. Their debts were to be settled in proper legal ways.

William was delighted at the ruling. He wrote to the LMS in London,

"I thank God for His gracious support through many days and nights of anxiety, enabling me with mildness yet steadfastness to oppose."[198]

Yet William knew that he needed to find practical ways to help the people avoid the temptation of alcohol. A few years later he founded a Temperance Society, a movement which fought alcohol abuse by educating people and promoting abstinence.

It had a dramatically beneficial effect in the area, but William faced strong criticism over it, even from religious quarters. Some of those opposed saw it as an attempt to restrict personal freedom.

"My support for the Temperance Society in no way lessens my belief that only the Word of God through the grace of God can really deliver people," he told the Dutch minister of George, Balloh. "In fact, all the efforts of the Society are based on the teaching of the Bible."

"I have too great a respect for the Word of God to consider such a Society necessary," replied Balloh rather superciliously, "and, what is more, I do not think it wise to interfere in the liberty of others."

William did not argue the point. Two weeks after this exchange, the parish clerk of Balloh's church got so drunk on a

Saturday night that he was unable to perform his duty the next day.

William commented to Johanna,

"The man was not only under the preached word but also read the Word of God on Sundays to others. Despite all this, it seems he could well have benefited from the help of our Temperance Society."

In 1828, the Cape government implemented new laws that seemed to give the Khoikhoi legal equality with the whites. Ordinance 50 released Khoikhoi of the Colony from having to carry passes, and gave inhabitants of Pacaltsdorp freedom to leave the settlement whenever they wanted, and they could legally own land. The new laws were in no small part due to the efforts and influence of missionaries.[199]

William was very happy with the fairer laws, but also reminded his congregation that they, too, needed to change their ways.

"It is one thing to have rights on paper. It is another to experience those rights in practice. This is why knowledge and education are so important, but even more important than any head knowledge . . . ," William paused to emphasise his point, ". . . is the influence of the Holy Spirit in our hearts. Only as we submit to His gracious influence, can we learn true wisdom and knowledge and begin to live righteous lives. Righteousness is the only cure for all the evils in society about which we so rightly complain."

William was not only concerned about seeing more of the Holy Spirit's work among his people in Pacaltsdorp. He also felt there was a 'deadness' among the missionaries at many LMS stations. He discussed it with Miles when he visited Pacaltsdorp.[200]

"Many of us can, with hard work, accomplish much. Things look good with buildings and programmes and all the rest. But what we really need, all the money and all the hard work on earth cannot produce," said William. "We need the gracious work and lasting fruit of the Holy Spirit to make our labours truly effective."

Miles nodded in agreement.

By then, William was sixty. He had been with the LMS in Africa for thirty years, and wondered how much more time he had left to serve his people. He still had some fighting to do.

---

[194] Briggs, Roy & Wing, Joseph: The Harvest and the Hope, UCCSA, Johannesburg, 1970, pp 33-37.

[195] CWM/LMS/05/02/02/033, Anderson to LMS, various letters 1827/8.

[196] CWM/LMS/05/02/02/033, Miles memorandum, 24 July 1827

[197] The 'Hottentot Code' proclamation of 1 November 1809, Cape Town

[198] Ibid, Anderson to Arundel of LMS, 13 November 1827

[199] Keegan, Timothy: Colonial South Africa and the Origins of the Racial Order, David Philip Publishers, Cape Town, 1996, p 103; see also Macmillan, W.H.: The Cape Colour Question, a Historical Survey, Cape Town, 1968, pp 213-19; and Cape of Good Hope Ordinances, 1828, Art 3, Ordinance 50.

[200] CWM/LMS/05/02/02/033, Anderson to LMS, 13 November, 1827

CHAPTER 30:

Haven of Hope

*D*uring the 1830s a number of violent and bloody clashes broke out in the eastern border areas of the Colony.

The Xhosa peoples, already under pressure from Zulu military expansion in Natal to their north, felt threatened by white settlers trying to establish themselves in the south. Despite the efforts of the government to keep the peace on the eastern frontier, Xhosa angry at losing more and more of their land attacked the colonists with increasingly ferocious raids. This resulted in the Sixth Frontier War of 1834-35, which took a heavy toll in life and property.[201]

Meanwhile, increasing dissatisfaction with the government and a feeling of insecurity among Afrikaner farmers in the border areas led to a movement that became known as the Great Trek. In an attempt to establish their own states outside of British control, some 15,000 Afrikaner frontier settlers left the Cape Colony and moved inland.

These were violent and bloody days in the history of South Africa.

Pacaltsdorp, by contrast, was a haven of hope. Despite a series of severe droughts and problems of drunkenness, poverty, disease, and periods of economic hardship, it became renowned for its schools, industry and general social order.

"Pacaltsdorp is one of those places on which the eyes look, and the thoughts dwell with peculiar feelings and associations," wrote one visitor. "Comparing what the place was when the mission was established with what it is now, it may well be said, 'what hath God wrought'."[202]

Another visitor was botanist and missionary James Backhouse, who undertook extensive travels in Australia and South Africa. "Pacaltsdorp has the aspect of an English village," he wrote, "and this is produced by the little 'church', with a single tower, and the white cottages of the missionary, schoolmaster, and schools." Backhouse was impressed by "the aged missionary William Anderson" and his family, and also by the industry of the local people. He describes Pacaltsdorp's inhabitants as "clean & smartly dressed especially when they went to attend public worship. . . Many of them have felt some measure of the power of the Gospel."[203]

Most families had private gardens in which they grew a great variety of vegetables. Some also grew crops such as wheat, oats, maize, potatoes, and tobacco. William himself encouraged the planting of trees such as oaks, firs, and poplars; as well as fruit trees, from apple, pear, fig, peach, and apricot, to almond, plum, lemon, mulberry, walnut, and pomegranate.

Many of the people kept sheep and cattle, some for breeding.

Others in Pacaltsdorp had developed trades such as wagon-making, carpentry, building, and shoe-making. Others were blacksmiths, tailors and timber cutters.

Whenever government dignitaries passed through the area, they would visit Pacaltsdorp. Governor Sir Lowry Cole was highly impressed during his visit in 1829,[204] as were later governors such as Sir George Napier in March 1838.

Napier and his Military Secretary, Major Chartries, were shown around the Infant School by Elizabeth, the Andersons' fourth daughter. She was by then an attractive twenty two-year-old brunette.

"Miss Anderson," said the Governor, surrounded by a mob of smiling children, "you and your helpers are doing a marvellous job. I doubt there is a school in Cape Town that could claim to be better than your school."

Elizabeth blushed.

"Your Excellency, my older sister Johanna laid the foundations for what I am doing, and we both owe a lot to our training under Miss Lyndale in Cape Town." [205]

The almost one hundred children in the Infant School had excelled themselves that day singing and reciting for the visitors. They obviously loved their teacher and wanted to do her proud.

Elizabeth and her siblings had become an important part of life in Pacaltsdorp. They were active in the church and Sunday School, and ran the Infant School and the highly successful Sewing and Industry School.

William's second oldest daughter, Catherina, was a gifted artist. He would often tell admiring friends that her artistic talent likely came from his own mother Catherine, who was a close relative of the famous English painter, Turner. Kitty, as she was known, was also dedicated to her work in the Sewing and Industry School. She loved the children and young people among whom she worked.

On one occasion, she came running, urgently calling for her father.[206] "Papa, one of my boys, Fredrick Roode, is very ill and wants to see you. He says he will not recover."

"Kitty, darling," replied William, "I will go right away."

Sitting by the twelve-year-old boy's bedside, accompanied by Kitty and a visitor, Captain Fawcett from India, William talked to Fredrick.

"Well, Fredrick, why did you send for me?"

"Because, sir, I'm going to leave you."

"Where do you think you are going, Fredrick?"

"To heaven, sir."

"And who is going to take you to heaven, Fredrick?" asked William with a growing lump in his throat.

"Jesus Christ, sir," replied Fredrick without hesitation.

"But aren't you a sinner, Fredrick?"

"Oh yes, sir. But God has forgiven my sins because Jesus died for sinners."

"That's wonderful, Fredrick," said William. He could see the little boy was very ill, yet remained cheerful and confident in his faith. He was amazed. "Do you want me to pray with you, then?" he continued.

"If you please, sir," came the happy reply.

After William left, Fredrick asked to see his schoolmates. He spoke to them solemnly but with no sense of regret.

"I can no longer play with you all. I am going soon. You must obey your parents. Do you remember the commandment 'Honour your father and mother'? I hope you will not steal anymore. It is a great sin before God."

He then quoted several Bible verses and urged his classmates to believe in Jesus. Finally, he shook hands with each one. Later in the evening, after his teacher Kitty had left, he called his family and said good-bye to his little sisters.

About midnight, he asked his father, who had him on his lap, to put him on his bed. He then told his mother,

"Mamma, I must leave you, God is calling me away. Give me the last kiss."

His parents' hearts were breaking, but after that kiss, all pain seemed to leave his little body. Shortly after, they heard him say,

"Lord Jesus, do receive me. I am a great sinner, but pardon my sins." Then he was gone.

William enjoyed his pastoral work, and marvelled at the way God worked in people's lives. They had regular baptisms in the church.

One baptism involved a man who had been an alcoholic and who had given so much trouble that he had been expelled from Pacaltsdorp. His conversion, and the dramatic change that followed in his life, caused a stir.

That morning, the man's daughter was also baptised, and his grand-daughter dedicated.

As William greeted people leaving the church after the baptisms, one of the members gripping William's hand said,

"Pastor, when I saw Class Slinger standing in front of the pulpit today, I could hardly believe my eyes."[207]

Such events made all the disappointments seem of little consequence to William.

The Anderson household was always humming with activity. The mission house was a large, though simple, double storey building. The Andersons often hosted visitors.

Love and romance were obviously in the air when Henry Helm's sons visited Pacaltsdorp in late 1834. They had come from the Caledon Institute in Zuurbraak where their parents were in charge, and where William and Johanna had first served following their sad departure from Griquatown in 1820.

By then, their youngest son Bartholomew was a teenager, and his sisters were attractive young women – and most eligible.

The Anderson girls went out distributing gospel tracts with Daniel Helm, who had his eyes on William's third daughter Johanna. It was a big occasion when she married Daniel at Pacaltsdorp on 11 June 1835.[208] Her mother wrote a poem for the young Johanna on that happy day.

"United in hand may you be so in heart,
May each with the other agree;
In joy or in sorrow, may each take a part,
And each a true yoke-fellow be.

Convinced that your interest now is but one,
Let your views and pursuits be the same;
And when by your means any good shall be done,
Give praise to Emmanuel's name.

To Him be your altar devoted each day,
On Him rest your cares every night;
From Him never venture one moment to stray,
But make His commands your delight."

The elder Johanna was an affectionate mother and much loved by all her children. She was a role model – for them and for the many others who knew her – in the way she taught her children and managed her busy household, as well as in the way she supported and worked with her husband. William knew he had a real partner in Johanna, and he prayed that his daughter would be just such a wife to Daniel.

Six years later, in February 1841, the Anderson's fourth daughter Elizabeth would marry another Helm boy, William.[209] The Andersons had always enjoyed a close relationship with the Helms, their children having played together in Griquatown, and William and Johanna were delighted to see two of their daughters marry into the Helm family.[210]

While there were times of great joy in Pacaltsdorp, life was not always easy for William. In 1834, he was accused of being 'Troubler and Disturber of the District' by some local colonists, and summoned to answer the charges in the local court in George.[211]

At the time, the government was considering a new law, the Vagrancy Act.[212] If passed, it would require all Khoikhoi in the Colony to be registered with details of their birth, place of residence, contract work, and other information. If they were found to be unregistered, they would be regarded as vagrants.

News of the proposed bill had caused panic among the Khoikhoi inhabitants of the Colony, prompting hundreds to flee to places like Pacaltsdorp. They feared the law would nullify the provisions of Ordinance 50 of 1828 which, on paper at least, had given equal rights to Khoikhoi.

In court, the prosecutor, acting on behalf of several angry colonists, asked William, "Mr Anderson, I have in my hands a copy of The South African Commercial Advertiser for June 7th this year. I presume you have seen it and are aware of the article to which I shall refer?"

"Yes, sir, I have seen the article," replied William. The Advertiser was the main newspaper in the Cape.

"Let me quote," continued the prosecutor. "'In the meantime the agitation and excitement produced throughout the Colony, by the mere rumour of this new ordinance, may give us some faint idea of what is likely to follow its enactment and operation in the hands of Field Cornets and Justices of the Peace.'"

He continued, " 'The people are flying in hundreds from their usual places of abode, and from service of farmers, to the missionary institutions, under the impression . . . that the ordinance will make them the slaves of the Boers for life. To the little village of Pacaltsdorp, already overstocked with inhabitants, upwards of 200 have already fled as to a city of refuge.' Mr Anderson, would you care to give an explanation as to this reference to Pacaltsdorp and as to the reasons for such an influx from neighbouring farms to your Institution?"

"I will be glad to," replied William without hesitation. "Let me begin by saying that I totally agree with the sentiments expressed in the article in the South African Commercial Advertiser. In fact, we have had over 400 flee to Pacaltsdorp. It has raised the numbers residing at our institution from 516 to 946."

He continued, "As to the reasons for such an influx, I believe it should be only too obvious. The proposed Vagrancy Act would require all Hottentots and blacks in the Colony to be registered as to birth, residence, contract work, etcetera, or else they would be regarded as vagrants. It affects every man, woman, and child at present in service or out of service in the Colony. The servant may remain with his present master on that master's terms . . ." William repeated the phrase for emphasis, "on that master's terms, if he please; but if he does not please, he may not leave in order to look for other employment, for if he does, he becomes a 'Vagrant'. This proposed bill is a disgrace."

"Mr Anderson, kindly answer my question and refrain from political comments if you can," interrupted the prosecutor.

"I repeat," persisted William, "the proposed bill is a disgrace. It is no wonder that under such a law the servant would feel he is little different from a slave. Thus, instead of alleviating the problem of vagrancy, this proposed bill has only compounded the problem and has generated fear and apprehension."

"Mr Anderson, is it true that you have encouraged the flight to your institution of Hottentots from their service on colonists' farms?"

"Certainly not! It is the proposed Vagrancy Bill that has caused this panic," replied William. "I would never encourage people to leave their jobs. My only plea is for our Hottentots and blacks to be treated fairly and with the respect due to all men, regardless of their colour of skin or language. Only when our white farmers treat their labourers in this way, will they have stable and happy work forces."

"Mr Anderson, can you prove that you have not been an instigator in this present crisis?"

"I can only say what I have said, and you will find hundreds of witnesses that this is what I have always said. In addition, I can show the court copies of my extensive correspondence concerning this issue with the Colonial government. I also have records of my face-to-face discussions with the late Acting Governor Colonel Wade."[213]

The charges against William were dismissed, as were similar charges brought against him a month later.

William told a group of church members who had been praying for him, "I am not afraid of these things. I regard it an honour that even as an old man I am privileged to contend for the oppressed indigenous people of this land. It is for them that I have devoted the best part of my life, and it is in their service that I have spent the past thirty-five years."

Some good had come out of the influx, despite the problems it brought to the Pacaltsdorp community, which had to house and help the extra families. Church services were packed and many more children benefited from the schools. Within a year, as the panic over the proposed Vagrancy Acts receded, some of those who had flocked to Pacaltsdorp moved back to their former places of residence, though many stayed. The law was eventually disallowed by the Home Government in England, much to William's delight.

Another victory came four years later, on 1 December 1838.

It was indeed a special day. Not only was it William's birthday, but it was also the day when all slaves in the Colony were made free men and women. Largely as a result of the influence of leaders in the evangelical movement, the British Parliament had in 1807 passed a law abolishing the slave trade. It was only much later, however, in 1833, that the Emancipation Act was passed. Existing slaves were to be set free after undergoing four to six years of apprenticeship.

On the day of emancipation in the Cape Colony, a special service of thanksgiving was held at Pacaltsdorp. William preached on Psalm 48:9-11,[214] praising God for His love, righteousness, and justice.

These were golden years for William and Johanna. Although they were kept busy with people coming to ask advice about all

233

kinds of problems, William wrote to the directors of the LMS in London,

"I have never experienced so much unity among the people. This lightens my load and makes my work so pleasant. We are seeing unusual blessing."

He added, "Please pray for us. I long to finish my course with joy and remain faithful to the end."[215]

William and Johanna were getting older. They did not know how much longer they would have in the service of the people they loved.

---

[201] le Cordeur, Basil A: The Occupations of the Cape, 1795-1854, from An Illustrated History of South Africa, Jonathan Ball Publishers, Johannesburg 1986, p 88.

[202] The Evangelical Magazine and Missionary Chronicle, January 1834, p 39 – quoting from a report by George Christie, LMS missionary to India, who visited Pacaltsdorp in 1831.

[203] Extracts from the Letters of James Backhouse, Part 7, published by Harvey and Darton, London, 1840, pgs 32-34. Backhouse visited Pacaltsdorp in November 1838.

[204] CWM/LMS/05/02/02/036, Anderson to LMS, 29 January, 1830

[205] CWM/LMS/05/02/02/050, Anderson to LMS, 12 September, 1838

[206] CWM/LMS/05/02/02/046, Catherina Anderson with her father's report, 2 February 1836.

[207] CWM/LMS/05/02/02/040, Anderson, 14 January, 1833

[208] CWM/LMS/05/02/02/044, Anderson to LMS, 30 September, 1835

[209] CWM/LMS/05/02/02/056, Anderson to Freeman (LMS), 10 September 1841

[210] Helm, Charles: The Helm Family History, 1999, pp 46-48.

[211] CWM/LMS/05/02/02/044, Anderson to LMS, 6 January, 1835

[212] Keegan, Timothy: Colonial South Africa and the Origins of the Racial Order, David Philip Publishers, Cape Town, 1996, pp 119-121.

[213] CWM/LMS/05/02/02/042, Anderson to LMS, 6 January 1835

[214] CWM/LMS/05/02/02/050, Pacaltsdorp Report, 1838

[215] CWM/LMS/05/02/02/058, Anderson to LMS, 4 December 1842

CHAPTER 31:

Passing The Baton

$\mathcal{T}$here was excited whispering as heads turned to watch the entrance of the bride. Looking stunningly beautiful, Janet walked slowly down the aisle of the crowded church, accompanied by her father John Melvill. She smiled the shy, nervous smile of a happy bride and tried to keep in time with the music. At the front stood Bartholomew, the youngest son of William and Johanna, waiting proudly. He was just a few weeks short of his twenty third-birthday.

The wedding was held in Dysselsdorp[216], a small settlement lying two days' journey over the Outeniqua mountains from Pacaltsdorp, where Melvill had been serving as resident missionary for four years. He had been appointed as government agent in Griquatown after William left, but had resigned later and joined the LMS.[217]

William conducted the marriage service, assisted by the bride's father.

During the simple reception held under the trees in the church garden, Bartholomew gave his bridegroom's speech. He told of how he had met Janet.

"My parents have long known my new father- and mother-in-law. Janet's parents served in Griquatown where I was born, but sadly it was after we had left. My parents tell me that Janet and I did meet in Cape Town in 1820, but that being twenty two years ago, it seems neither of us remember that meeting."

Everyone burst into laughter and clapped.

"I first became aware of this beautiful young lady," he said with a huge beam as he looked at her, "now Mrs B.E. Anderson, in January of 1838, when she and her family visited us here in Pacaltsdorp. I was only eighteen, but it was love at first sight. Of course I had to keep it secret, or my sisters would have given me no peace. At that time I was back for Christmas from Cape Town, where I was undergoing training as a carpenter builder. It was the most difficult thing to return to Cape Town after having just met Janet. Later, when back in Pacaltsdorp, on the occasions when my father had to travel to Dysselsdorp, I made sure he took me with him. I didn't let on why, of course."

Following their marriage, Bartholomew and Janet made their home in Pacaltsdorp, and just over a year later, in October 1843, their first child, Anna Fredrika, was born. In 1844, the young family moved to Dysselsdorp to assist the Melvills in their work. There, Bartholomew took on the role of headmaster of the mission school.

Bartholomew was later to take over from his father-in-law when Melvill's failing eyesight compelled him to retire. The dry, often dusty, atmosphere of the Little Karoo aggravated his condition.

The work in Dysselsdorp, though only a few years old, was flourishing. The school was going well and Sunday worship services were well-attended. Bartholomew not only lived by his trade and ran the school, he also preached widely in the district, as far as the town of Oudtshoorn and the Cango Caves.[218]

His older brother Johannes had also trained as a builder and was living in George. Unlike his siblings, however, Johannes did not show much interest in spiritual things, even though he respected his parent's faith. William and Johanna longed for him to turn to the Lord, but they knew it had to be his own choice.

Johannes had been at a very impressionable age when his parents faced their hardest years in Griquatown and when the difficulties with his father's colleague James Read came to a head. It had left much hurt in his young heart and mind.

Bartholomew's growing effectiveness as a preacher was a special encouragement to William and Johanna as they grew increasingly weak themselves. William had long supported his son in his desire to become a missionary with the LMS, and was overjoyed when the directors finally accepted him. They had been reluctant at first because he had no formal theological training.

Ordination was a further hurdle. Bartholomew could not baptise, lead communion, or solemnise marriages in Dysselsdorp unless he was ordained. Clericalism was a problem even in the LMS, despite the Society having stressed the role of the laity when it was founded. Dysselsdorp's growing church decided to write a petition urging Dr Philip, the LMS Superintendent, to approve Bartholomew's ordination. It was signed by over 200 people.[219]

Dr Philip agreed to the ordination, and an ordination service was held in the Pacaltsdorp church on Friday 5 May 1848. It drew a large crowd, not only from George and Pacaltsdorp but also from several other places. Those attending included five LMS missionaries as well as students and staff of the new LMS Seminary at Hankey, close to Bethelsdorp and Port Elizabeth.

Dr Philip preached from 2 Corinthians 5:18, focusing on the solemn responsibility being given to Bartholomew, 'the ministry of reconciliation'. Several others took part in the service including Thomas Durant Philip, the son of Dr Philip, Reinhold Gregorowski, a young LMS missionary previously with the Berlin Missionary Society, and Thomas Hood. In a letter to the

LMS directors in London, Thomas Philip described the moving service.[220]

"Two that took part in the service were remarkably alike for age, length of service, honour, and appearance. The Rev W Anderson, the father of the young man, was one of those missionaries that left England for the Cape in 1800, and has never since that period, revisited his own country. He is not far from reaching his eighties and his conversation is rich in recollections of those days of the Society's history which seem, to us young ones, to belong to another age. It was truly a season of thankfulness for the old man to see his son consecrated to the same service," wrote the younger Philip.

"His voice naturally trembled more from emotion than from age as he laid his hands upon the head of his son and implored of God the richest outpouring of grace to fit him for the ministry to which God had called him.

Dr Philip was the other, who is a few years younger than Mr Anderson, and like him, living daily and hourly in expectation of that call which shall summon him to enter into the joy of his Lord."

At the end of the letter, Thomas Philip asked for as many good theological books as possible to be sent to Bartholomew, who had not received the same education as most ministers and missionaries sent from England. Being eager to advance his education, Bartholomew was very grateful to Thomas Philip for his support. The fact remained, however, that despite his youth and lack of formal theological education, Bartholomew was already becoming a powerful preacher and much-loved pastor to his people. He knew the Scriptures a good deal better than many who had been through theological training.

William and Johanna were increasingly feeling their age. Two years before Bartholomew's ordination, William had written to

Dr Philip asking to be released from the secular concerns of the institution.[221] He was aware that he could not keep up.

"The work and responsibilities are too wearying for me," he explained, "and the population is very large and requires an efficiency of exertion and activity which is beyond my strength."

Help was eventually sent in the form of Gregorowski and his wife.[222] William was able to hand over much of the day-to-day affairs of the institution to them.

Now, a few years later, he felt he should retire from his spiritual responsibilities as well. He had been ill and could not concentrate on anything for long.

"I am conscious," William wrote, "that much deficiency and imperfection has attended my very best service leaving me nothing to boast of except the mercy and faithfulness of a kind and gracious God who has preserved me amid many a thousand snares and temptations and has supported me under many difficulties and delivered me in times of great danger."

He added, "I have done so little for my dear Redeemer."[223]

It was on Thursday, 22 June 1848, just over a month after his son's ordination, that William faced one of his greatest trials.[224] Johanna, who had been weak for some time became so ill that she needed to be confined to bed. After a week, her condition suddenly and unexpectedly deteriorated. Her speech failed her and, much to William's distress, she sank into unconsciousness.

He stayed by her side throughout this time, and when he realised she was finally gone, he lay against her body, gently holding her close, and sobbed.

"Johanna, my darling, you are gone. You were my constant companion and support. You always loved me and always loved our blessed Saviour with all your heart. How can I live without you? Oh Johanna, my darling, I need you. I love you."

William felt her loss deeply, but never doubted that his beloved partner of forty-two years was now with her Lord and

Saviour whom she had served so devotedly. He had a beautiful inscription carved on her grave stone:

"Shining in all the graces of a Christian, she discharged with fidelity every duty and prayerfully sought to improve every opportunity of usefulness among her fellow creatures till she fell asleep in Jesus."

Rev Theophilus Atkinson and his wife had come to relieve William of his work. By now, William was seventy-eight, and after Johanna's death, his own health seemed to deteriorate. He soon gave up preaching, never to enter the pulpit again, although he remained interested in everything that was happening at Pacaltsdorp. He regularly attended the Sunday services, and was always keen to hear about the work of the LMS and other missions around the world. He was so eager to continue receiving the Missionary Chronicle and other publications sent to Pacaltsdorp –which he used for prayer – that Atkinson had to ask the LMS to send an extra copy. Atkinson realised that the old man would not take kindly to losing the privilege of receiving his own copy.[225]

William spent much of his time praying and reading the Bible, which became increasingly precious to him.

"It gives me all the comfort and strength I need," he told his daughter Kitty. "I am now awaiting the call of my Master."

When he turned eighty-two, William wrote a short poem, "On the Pleasures of Religion". He was not thinking of non-Christian religions nor of nominal or cultural Christianity. For him, "religion" referred to a living, personal relationship with Jesus Christ.

'Tis Religion that can give
Sweetest pleasures while we live.
'Tis Religion must supply
Solid comfort when we die.

After Death its joys will be
Lasting as Eternity.
Be the living God thy friend
Then your bliss shall never end.

The poem was prefaced with a quotation from Proverbs 3:17, "And her ways are ways of pleasantness, and all her paths are peace."[226]

On 3 September 1851, Dr John Philip died in Hankey, where he had been living in retirement with his son Thomas. William deeply respected Dr Philip and the two men had been close friends.

James Read, who had arrived in Africa on the same ship as William, also died the same year. After being embroiled in various scandals, including adultery, and being eventually restored, he had served in the unsettled areas of the eastern border among the Xhosa. He and his son, also called James, had been active in pressing for the rights of the Khoikhoi and other indigenous peoples in southern Africa. Both men, father and son, had even travelled to England in 1835 as part of a delegation to give evidence before a Select Committee of the British Parliament.[227]

Read's passing was sad news for William. He had always regarded him as a colleague and friend, and bore no bitterness over Read's actions in trying to discredit him in the eyes of the Griqua captains.

The following year, in August 1852, Bartholomew and Janet were urgently called to George, where Janet's father, John Melvill, had been doing Christian work. Melvill had died after suffering a stroke.[228]

After conducting the funeral, at which he preached a powerful sermon in the crowded chapel, Bartholomew decided to stay in Pacaltsdorp rather than return to his work in Dysselsdorp. Janet stayed on in George to accompany her mother. Bartholomew knew that his own father was nearing his 'home call'.

"Bartholomew, I am soon to leave you," William told his son. Both he and Bartholomew knew he was dying. "My boy, will you stay here with me until my Saviour calls me home?"

Bartholomew took his father's hand and assured him he would. Although it would mean being away from his work for some time, he felt that staying with his father now would be the right thing to do.

Early in his illness, there were a number of times when William struggled with depression, but his 'gloomy thoughts', as he called them, did not last long. His mind was now clear, and his heart at peace.

"God is so good. He does not lay more upon us than He will enable us to bear," he said to Maria and Kitty, the two oldest girls. "May He give me faith and patience to hear His will. I want to glorify Him in the furnace, for those He loves, He disciplines."

The children took turns to be with their father. He often talked of his confidence in Christ and sang or quoted his favourite hymns.

> "Jesus, the vision of Thy face
> Hath over-powering charms
> Scarce shall I feel death's cold embrace
> If I be in Christ's arms."

On 11 September, two weeks after his serious illness began, William gathered his children. At times he seemed to be talking to them, at other times, he was obviously praying.

"I lie at the foot of the Cross repenting," he said, "my only hope is in Christ. The enemy of souls is busy, but I fear him not. I see no hope of my recovery and I do not wish for it. Jesus is an almighty Saviour; oh, my dear Saviour, come and be with me. Let me enjoy Your special presence."

In the evening, he called them all again and spoke first to Bartholomew.

"My son, God has called you to the work of the ministry. Be faithful to the end. Farewell. Give my love to your people."

Then, turning to the girls, he said, "My dear children, I am going to leave you. I die trusting in Christ for salvation. Farewell. The Lord bless you. Continue to walk in the fear of the Lord."

For the next few days, however, William held on to life and remained alert. At times, he simply lay on his bed praying out loud.

"Oh my Saviour, You are my all in all, my Redeemer, my advocate, my hope, and joy."

He asked for Isaac Watts' hymn, 'There is a land of pure delight', to be recited for him, and after listening to the words, said,

"Beautiful lines. Yes, I see that land with the eye of faith. I have long wished to depart."

He began to sing another of Watts' hymns.

> "Why was I made to hear Thy voice,
> And enter while there's room;
> When thousands make a wretched choice,
> And rather starve than come.
>
> 'Twas the same love that spread the feast,
> That sweetly forced me in;
> Else we had still refused to taste,
> And perished in our sin."

William was getting weaker. He thought of all his dear people, the Griqua and the people of Pacaltsdorp.

"Tell the people," he said to Bartholomew, "that the same word I preached to them is now my support. Tell them that Christ is all in all. They must look to Him alone for salvation."

By now, he was having terrible chest pains which left him breathless. After one such attack, Bartholomew asked,

"Father, how are you feeling now?"

"I'm very happy. I rejoice in the hope that I shall soon see my Saviour."

Soon after, another attack deprived him of speech, and breathing became very difficult. William's children strained to hear as he tried to speak. They could just make out the words:

"Jordan stream – mercy – eternal life."

Several hours later, William Anderson gently breathed his last. It was Friday, 24 September 1852. He was a few months short of his eighty third birthday.[229]

The following Monday, a large congregation filled the great stone church in Pacaltsdorp. Among those gathered for William's funeral were most of the people of Pacaltsdorp, many from George, including leading citizens, local farmers and people from further afield. Hundreds stood outside, unable to squeeze into the building.

As Bartholomew saw the respect shown for his father by all races and ranks of people, he was overcome with emotion. He said of his father,

"As a minister of the Gospel, he was plain and unassuming, but faithful and zealous. As a pastor, he was kind and affectionate, but at the same time commanded respect from all. He knew his people, both Griqua and the people of Pacaltsdorp, very well and although faithful at all times to point out their faults, he fearlessly advocated their rights."[230]

William had served in Africa for over fifty years.

A lengthy tribute was published in the major newspaper of the Cape, the South African Commercial Advertiser on 2 October 1852. Commenting on William's life, the writer said,

"Mr Anderson was a man of good natural abilities, of indomitable courage, and boundless benevolence. His name is revered by the races whom he first led into the paths of civilized life, by pouring upon their minds the light of the eternal world. Within the Colony, where he has long pursued his chosen labours, he was equally esteemed and revered by all classes of people, to whose respect and confidence his singleness of purpose and upright character never failed to recommend him."[231]

William was buried next to Johanna in Pacaltsdorp. Though she was of Dutch and Huguenot descent, her tombstone was in English. William's, at his request, was in Dutch – one further testimony to his lifelong calling to promote peace and reconciliation through Christ.

That night, after the funeral, Bartholomew knelt by his bed and prayed,

"Oh Lord, what great things You accomplished through father and mother, and other pioneer missionaries. May we learn from them. What trials and difficulties are still awaiting Your servants in Africa! May we not be discouraged. I only pray that a double portion of the Spirit that rested on our parents, in whose steps we are now treading, may rest upon us."

William's death marked the passing of an era, but he had left behind a legacy of faith and love that speaks to every generation. It is small wonder that this story has no ending.

---

[216] Dr Charles Helm in The Helm Family History (page 49) records, "Theirs is the first entry in the well-preserved marriage register" in Dysselsdorp.

[217] Briggs, Roy & Wing, Joseph: The Harvest and the Hope, UCCSA, Johannesburg, 1970, p 53.

[218] CWM/LMS/05/02/02/064, Anderson to LMS, 17 October, 1845

[219] CWM/LMS/05/02/02/068, Anderson to LMS, 30 October, 1847

[220] CWM/LMS/05/02/02/070, T Philip to LMS, 11 May, 1848

[221] CWM/LMS/05/02/02/064, Anderson to LMS, 24 January, 1845

[222] Anderson, T.A.: The Story of Pacaltsdorp and Some Reminiscences, George, 1957, pp 37, 38.

[223] CWM/LMS/05/02/02/070, Anderson to LMS, 30 October, 1847

[224] Ibid, Anderson to LMS, 1 September, 1848

[225] CWM/LMS/05/02/02/074, Atkinson to LMS, 17 April, 1850
[226] Helm, Charles: The Helm Family History, 1999, p 36.
[227] le Cordeur, Basil A: The Occupations of the Cape, 1795-1854, from An Illustrated History of South Africa, Jonathan Ball Publishers, Johannesburg 1986, p83.
[228] CWM/LMS/05/02/02/079, Atkinson to LMS, 27 August, 1852
[229] CWM/LMS/05/02/02/079, B.E. Anderson to LMS, 23 December, 1852
[230] Ibid.
[231] South African Commercial Advertiser, 2 October 1852, Cape Town, National Library of South Africa, Microfilm Collection, MP1031, Reel 23.

B.E. Anderson

Postscript

*W*hen William Anderson offered himself to the LMS for service in Africa, he would never have imagined the legacy his life of selfless service to Christ would leave to future generations.

Three of the Anderson girls, Maria, 'Kitty', and Wilhemina, remained happily single and became well-respected educators in Swellendam, where they settled after William's death. Johanna and her husband Daniel Helm served at the Caledon Institute in Zuurbraak, where they succeeded Daniel's father Henry Helm. Their son Charles became one of the earliest missionaries to work in Matabeleland, Zimbabwe. Another son, Sam, worked with the LMS in Grahamstown.

Bartholomew worked at Dysselsdorp till 1862, then became minister of the Congregational Church in Oudtshoorn. This church grew into one of the largest in South Africa, with a multi-racial congregation that at one point numbered over 2700. After twelve years of happy marriage, his wife Janet Melvill died in a tragic accident. She was just thirty-five years old and pregnant with their sixth child when she fell off a horse.[232]

Their son, Ebenezer Tom (ET), married Frances Kayser, daughter of Henry Kayser, a German missionary of the LMS. ET became a well-known magistrate. Bartholomew remarried and had two more sons, Charles and George, with his second wife Georgina Elliot. Both became accomplished doctors in Cape Town. Bartholomew himself died in 1900.

When a memorial service for Bartholomew was held nineteen years after his death, marking the 100th anniversary of his birth, it was attended by some 2000 people. Clearly, the Andersons' youngest son had made a great impact on those to whom he ministered.

Many of William and Johanna's descendants have served – and still serve – in missionary or pastoral work in a variety of Christian denominations, in southern Africa and overseas. Others have been teachers, doctors, engineers, or businessmen. Not all, but most, have shared the strong Christian commitment of William and Johanna.

Indeed, through eight generations, the truth of the biblical promise – that God's love and faithfulness blesses succeeding generations of 'those who love Him and keep His commands' – has been demonstrated.

I am one of those so blessed, being a sixth-generation descendant of William and Johanna through Bartholomew and Janet Melvill, and their son Ebenezer Tom. Ebenezer and Frances' son, William Wardlaw Anderson, my own grandfather, served as a missionary of the LMS in Zimbabwe for almost fifty years.

Throughout his life, William Anderson longed for people of different languages and cultures to live in harmony and mutual respect. He fought for righteousness, love, and peace; hence the title of this book 'Weapons of Peace'.

This biblical message rings as urgently in the Twenty-first Century as it did in the Nineteenth Century.

William's on-going story also shows that any work of love, faith, and service can ride out the storms of history. Over two hundred years after he first preached to the Korana and Griqua north of the Orange River, the church William started among them is alive and well, as is the church he and Johanna served in Pacaltsdorp.

Further illustration of the enduring value of the sacrificial sharing of God's love with others came to me one day as I was doing research in the library of London University's School of African and Oriental Studies. I had been reading the accounts of the historic meetings between Tswana Chief Mothibi and LMS missionaries William Anderson, John Campbell, and James Read. There were no known Tswana Christians at the time.

That day in 1991, in SOAS library, one hundred and eighty years later, I met one. He was a university professor who was also an ordained minister. He was a Tswana, one of the many radiant Tswana Christians today. The seeds sown in tears by William and his LMS colleagues have yielded a rich harvest.

What has not survived the passage of time is that great evangelical movement, the London Missionary Society. Some of its workers became famous, among them Robert Moffat and David Livingstone in Africa; and Robert Morrison and Griffith John in China. But there were thousands of little-sung heroes, too.

The LMS as an organisation is no more, having been merged with the Congregational Council for World Mission. But the message of its founders and its workers, including William and Johanna Anderson, will never cease to be relevant, for it is the message of God's love for a lost mankind.

---

[232] Helm, Charles: The Helm Family History, 1999, p 51.

Governors at the Cape
1795 - 1852

First British Occupation, 1795 - 1803
General James Henry Craig, 1795 - May 1797
First British Military Governor, Earl Macartney, 1797/8
Major-General Francis Dundas, 1798 - 1803; Sir George Yonge (Governor December 1800 - April 1801)

The Batavian (Dutch) Occupation, 1803 - 1806
Military Governor, Jan Willem Janssens

The Second British Occupation, 1806 - 1814
Sir David Baird, 1806 - 1807 (acting)
General H G Grey, 1807 (acting)
Earl of Caledon, 1807 - 1811
General Robert Meade, 1813 - 1814 (acting)
Sir John Francis Cradock, 1811 - 1814

Following the London Convention of 13 August 1814, when the Dutch permanently ceded the Cape to Great Britain
Lord Charles Somerset, 1814 - 1826
Sir Rufane Donkin, 1820 - 1821 (acting)
General Richard Bourke, 1826 - 1828 (acting)
Sir Lowry Cole, 1828 - 1833
Colonel T F Wade, 1833 - 1834 (acting)
Sir Benjamin D'Urban, 1834 - 1838
Sir George Napier, 1838 - 1844
Sir Peregrine Maitland, 1844 - 1847
Sir Henry Pottinger, 1847
Sir Harry Smith, 1847 - 1852

Glossary and Notes

Assegai:	Spear, either short, for stabbing, or long, for throwing.
'Bastards':	Name by which Griqua were originally known, until John Campbell suggested the change.
Batavia:	Colony ruled by Dutch East India Company in Java (present-day Indonesia) from which slaves were brought to the Cape in the eighteenth century.
Batavian Republic:	French satellite administration ruling Holland and its colonies in the period following the overthrow of the Dutch monarchy by Napoleon Bonaparte.
Boer:	Literally meaning 'farmer', it refers to descendants of Dutch colonists who settled in the Cape.
Burgher:	Dutch term meaning 'citizen'.
Bushman:	Term used by Dutch settlers at Cape for hunter-gatherers indigenous to southern Africa.
Cape of Good Hope:	Peninsula of land stretching from Table Mountain to Cape Point, named by Portuguese sailors in the fifteenth century; area settled by the Dutch in the seventeenth and eighteenth centuries; British Colony - eventually extending north to the Orange River and east to the KwaZulu-Natal border.
Carey:	William Carey, regarded by many as the 'founder of the modern missionary movement'; his writing and preaching led to the setting up of the Baptist Missionary Society in October, 1792, and the following year he left for India as a missionary remaining there till his death in 1834. His work included Bible translation, evangelism, the establishing of churches, educational and medical institutions, as well as social reform and horticultural research.
Coloured:	Person of mixed descent.
De Kaap:	Dutch name for early settlement at Table Bay, later called Cape Town.
Difaqane:	see Mfecane.
Dominee:	Dutch for minister of religion, ordained clergy – also called 'predikant'.
Dorp:	Small village or town.

Dutch East India Company:	Dutch trading company with extensive interests in the 'spice islands' of the East, which established a 'refreshment station' for passing ships at the Cape of Good Hope in the seventeenth century. It was dissolved in 1798.
1820 Settlers:	Groups of emigrant families from Britain, totalling approximately 1000 men and 3000 women and children, recruited by the British government, who settled in the eastern border areas of the Cape Colony in 1820.
Great Trek:	Migration in 1835,36 of Dutch speaking farmers mainly from the eastern border areas of the Cape who wanted to set up their own independent 'Boer republics' outside the borders of the Cape Colony.
Griqua:	People of mixed Khoikhoi, European, and other ancestry who settled mainly in the area of the Orange River; the focus of the missionary work of William and Johanna Anderson up till 1820. By the 1830's the Griqua had formed two factions, one under the Waterboers (Andries and his son Nicholas) at Griquatown, and the other under the Adam Koks (the second & third) at Philippolis. By the middle of the century the area of the Orange was in turmoil as Griqua, Voortrekkers, and British jostled for land which was also claimed by Sotho, Tswana, and other indigenous groups. The Griqua under Kok at Philippolis lost their land to the Boers and in 1862 moved east of the Drakensburg mountains to an area between the Cape and Natal, eventually founding the town of Kokstad. Major change came to the area known as Griqualand West controlled by Waterboer following the discovery of diamonds in 1867. This diamond-rich area, though long occupied by the Griqua, was claimed by the Boer republic of the Orange Free State, the South African Republic, and by the Cape Colony. Griqualand West was annexed by the British in 1871. Meanwhile the Griqua in Griqualand East, around Kokstad, despite stern resistance, also lost their independence when Britain annexed the area in 1879.
Hottentot:	Term used by early white settlers at the Cape for cattle-keeping indigenous people of southern Africa, known also as Khoikhoi.
Huguenots:	French refugees who settled in the Cape in the years following 1688 after fleeing religious persecution in Europe.

Karoo:	Means 'dry land', a term originating from Khoikhoi, used to refer to the drier areas in between the ranges of the Cape fold mountains (Little Karoo) and north beyond the mountains (Great Karoo).
Khoikhoi:	Literally 'men of men', cattle herders who inhabited southern Africa.
Kloof:	Mountain pass, ravine, or gorge.
Knobkerrie:	Stick with knob-like end used as a club.
Koranna:	A tribe of Khoikhoi. In the eighteenth and early nineteenth centuries found mostly in the area of the Orange River.
Landdrost:	Highest local government official in a given district (drostdy), magistrate.
LMS:	The London Missionary Society. Founded in London in September, 1795. Originally inter-denominational including both free churches ('non-conformist'), such as Congregationalists, as well as Anglicans and Presbyterians. Its 'sole object to spread the knowledge of Christ among the heathen and other unenlightened nations'. The LMS sent out tens of thousands of missionaries all over the world in the 150 years following its founding. Early on in its history, as other denominations founded their own societies, it became a largely Congregational movement. In the 1960s it was merged with the Congregational Council for World Mission.
Mfecane:	Upheaval in sub-continent of Africa in 1820-30s sparked by Zulu expansion, and leading to wide-spread inter-tribal warfare.
Mijnheer:	Dutch word for Mister.
Moravians:	A movement founded by Count Zinzendorf in Germany that saw hundreds of missionaries (most of whom were skilled artisans) sent out all over the world in the early eighteenth century. George Schmidt was the first Moravian to come to South Africa in 1737. He founded the Baviaans Kloof Mission (later called Genadendal), the first mission station in southern Africa. Schmidt taught the Khoikhoi to read and write and also to plant and sow, and baptised his first converts in 1742 but being a layman faced criticism from some clergy in the Netherlands. He returned to Amsterdam in 1744.

Non-conformist:	Evangelicals in England in the seventeenth to nineteenth centuries, who preferred to remain outside the official or state church (i.e. the Church of England). They included Congregationalists, Baptists, and Methodists, etc. In the seventeenth century 'non-conformists' (also known as 'dissenters') were often persecuted – e.g. John Bunyan's imprisonment in Bedford Prison, where he wrote the classic 'Pilgrim's Progress'.
Orange River:	Major river flowing east to west across southern Africa, from the Drakensberg mountains and entering the Atlantic Ocean north of the Kamies mountains; known by the Khoikhoi as Gariep (Great River); given the name Orange in 1777 by Col. Gordon, the Commander of the Dutch garrison at the Cape, in honour of the Royal Dutch House of Orange.
Ordinance 50:	A law passed in the Cape in 1828 that guaranteed to all "Hottentots and persons of colour" residing in the Cape the same freedom and protection as that enjoyed by whites.
Quagga:	An animal similar to the zebra but differing in its markings, once found in great numbers in southern Africa but which through hunting became extinct.
Rixdollar:	The monetary unit at the Cape first issued by the Dutch East India Company. In 1806 it was worth two English shillings – about a day's wage. In 1824 the rixdollar was replaced by British currency.
San:	See 'Bushman".
Trekboer:	Nomadic pastoral farmer, usually of Dutch extraction.
The S.A. Society:	The South African Society for Promoting the Spread of Christ's Kingdom; was formed in the Cape following the arrival of the first LMS recruits led by Dr J.T. van der Kemp in March, 1799. Enthusiastic support for the new society by the Dutch Reformed Church in the Cape and by LMS directors in London. The Society became the local representative of the LMS and the Netherlands Missionary Society.
Tswana:	Black peoples consisting of several tribes, speaking a similar language, that formed various confederations, living largely north of the Orange River in south central Africa. Like the Zulu and Xhosa, engaged in both pastoral and agricultural pursuits.

Xhosa: Black nation comprising various tribes and clans inhabiting south-east southern Africa. From the late 1700s the Xhosa and white settlers frequently clashed in their struggle for control of the rich grazing lands of the eastern Cape.

Zulu: Collective name for a group of black tribes, largely east of the Drakensberg mountains (present day KwaZulu-Natal) and north of the Xhosa-speaking peoples. The Zulu became a powerful unified nation under the Zulu king Shaka in the 1820s.

Tribute to William Anderson
in The South African Commercial Advertiser,
2 October 1852

(The full text of the tribute, printed below, was kindly supplied by
the National Library of South Africa, Cape Town. It is available in their
Microfilm Collection, MP1031, Reel 23)

The death of the Rev. William Anderson, which took
place on the 24th. at Pacaltsdorp, in the district of George,
carries the mind back to what may be called an early period
of the history of this Colony, when the country, a long way
on this side of the Orange River, was scarcely inhabited,
and the whole country immediately beyond it, where the
Griquas, the people of the Sovereignty, and the Emigrant
Boers, are now growing into prosperous communities, was
traversed only by wild beasts and savages scarcely less wild
or ferocious. Into this dark region Mr. Anderson and Mr.
Kramer penetrated more than half a century ago, at the risk
of their lives, for the noble purpose of reclaiming a miserable
race, which had sunk as low as perhaps it is possible for
human nature to descend. They were wanderers, living on
the precarious resources of nature in the fields, suffering
and inflicting on one another the extremities of savage
violence. Their misery and their vices only strengthened
the resolution of the missionary to devote his life to their
redemption, and after accompanying a single tribe in
their incessant migrations, for no less than five years, he
succeeded in persuading them to settle on a spot where
they could rear cattle and cultivate small portions of
ground. This step being gained, his work prospered far
beyond his most sanguine expectations, and the traveller
who now visits Griqua Town or Philipolis, if he has the
means of comparing the condition of the inhabitants in

1852 with what it was in 1800, will have no doubt, if he ever doubted, of the possibility of reclaiming a savage race by the force of Christianity.

Mr. Anderson was a man of good natural abilities, of indomitable courage, and boundless benevolence. His name is revered by the races who he first led into the paths of civilized life, by pouring upon their minds the light of the eternal world. Within the Colony, where he has long pursued his chosen labours, he was equally esteemed and revered by all classes of people, to whose respect and confidence his singleness of purpose and upright character never failed to recommend him.

The following letter from one who has long been associated with him in his labours, and the subjoined extract from the work of the Rev. Dr. Philip, will be read with peculiar interest, as they set forth in a lively manner, the nature of his primitive toils in the service of his Master, in the most arduous and at first sight least promising of fields :—

"Pacaltsdorp, Sept. 27, 1852.

"I have the melancholy task of communicating to you the tidings of the death of the Rev. William Anderson, who departed this life on Friday, the 24th instant.

"Our departed friend was born in London, on the 1st December, 1769, and was consequently nearly 83 years of age. He arrived in this colony in the year 1800, as a Missionary, in connection with the London Missionary Society, and continued faithfully and zealously to labour in this sacred cause, till in 1848 his increasing infirmities compelled him reluctantly to retire from active duties. For about 21 years he was engaged in missionary labours among the Griquas and other tribes to the north of the Orange River. During that long period he was called to endure many hardships, and to encounter numerous difficulties, arising from various sources. But supported by the grace of God, constrained by the love of Christ, and urged on by an earnest desire to promote the welfare and the eternal salvation of his fellow-men, he, in company with his beloved and lamented partners and fellow-labourers, held on in his arduous work, – and their faithful exertions were followed with a large measure of success.

"In the beginning of the year 1822 he was appointed to the superintendence of the Institution at Pacaltsdorp, where his labours for the temporal and spiritual interests of the people of his charge have been honoured by the Great Head of the Church with eminent success. By his instrumentality many have been turned from sin to righteousness. Some of these have gone before their aged pastor to the realms of bliss, and have doubtless welcomed him to their everlasting habitations. And many more are treading (it is believed) the way of life, who, with gratitude to God, regard our lamented brother as the minister by whom they believed, and who directed their feet into the ways of peace. His memory will long be cherished in the hearts of his attached and now mourning family and flock.

"The health of our venerable friend had long been declining, but he was generally able to attend public worship in the forenoon of the Sabbath, till within about two months of his decease. During the last month, however, his strength rapidly declined. He suffered much at times from oppression on his chest, which often deprived him of rest, and occasioned him many sleepless and wearisome nights. But he was mercifully sustained under his afflictions by that gracious God, whom he had so long endeavoured to serve in the Gospel of his Son. He was enabled to rely with unshaken confidence on Christ, his Saviour. His last communicable thoughts were fixed on 'the everlasting covenant,' made by God with his people, through his beloved Son; and his last intelligible words were of 'mercy' and 'everlasting life.' And thus he closed his long and holy and useful career with 'looking for the mercy of the Lord Jesus Christ unto eternal life.' And this passage of Scripture he had mentioned some months previous to his last illness as the text from which he wished his successor to improve the event of his death.

"His funeral took place on Monday, the 27th. and a large concourse of people assembled to pay the last public token of respect to this honoured servant of God. Many of the most respectable inhabitants of George were present on the solemn occasion, together with all the residents of the Institution, and many from other places. The service was conducted in the church, which was completely crowded. The 9oth Psalm and a portion of 1 Thessal. iv. were read, and an address delivered by the Rev. T. Atkinson, and prayer offered by the Rev. W. Elliott."

———

(The tribute in the SA Commercial Advertiser continues with a lengthy quotation from "Researches in South Africa, Volume 2", by Dr John Philip, which was published in London in 1828)

In the year 1800, when Mr. Anderson went among the Griquas, (as they are now denominated), they were a herd of wandering and naked savages, subsisting by plunder and the chase. Their bodies were daubed with red paint, their heads loaded with grease and shining powder; with no covering but the filthy kaross over their shoulders, without knowledge, without morals, or any traces of civilization, they were wholly abandoned to witchcraft, drunkenness, licentiousness, and all the consequences which arise from the unchecked growth of such vices. With his fellow labourer, Mr. Kramer, Mr. A. wandered about with them five years and a half, exposed to all the dangers and privations inseparable from such a state of society, before they could induce them to locate where they are now settled.

The country possessed by this people is not so favourable to agriculture as many districts in the colony, and in its present state it is not in a condition to support its increasing population by the cultivation of the earth alone; but the Griquas have now as a good a title to be considered as agricultural people as any class in the colony at a remote distance from Cape Town. I did not see in my late journey, a single fountain in the whole of this country unoccupied; and to show the eagerness of the people to avail themselves of every opportunity that can facilitate agricultural pursuits, they are now employed in attempting to lead out the Great Orange river over a large plain contiguous to English Drift. The difficulties of this undertaking are truly appalling, and would have deterred perhaps nine-tenths of the inhabitants of the colony from the attempt: and much as I wish them success, I am doubtful of the issue; but the attempt itself indicates a very great change for the better, when compared with their former habit of life. One of the leading literary journals of the present day, when speaking of the improvements made by missionaries in another quarter of the globe, remarks, "But we may drop all other considerations; this along, – the advancement of a people from the pastoral to the agricultural state, is the greatest and most important step in civilization."

When the labours of the missionaries began to produce their legitimate effects on the minds of the Griquas, promiscuous intercourse between the sexes was instantly abandoned, and since that period, every man has confined himself to one wife. The state of polygamy, as it exists among savage tribes, is one of the greatest obstacles to the success of the missionaries; and when the Christian religion operates so powerfully upon their minds, as to enable them to make the sacrifice which its abandonment requires, the missionaries are furnished with one of the most unquestionable evidences of the efficacy of the instrument they employ, and have the best securities for the future triumph of their principles.

As a corroboration of the proceeding statement, the following extract of a letter from the Rev. Wm. Anderson, formerly of Griqua Town, and now of Pacaltsdorp, dated 23d December 1825, will be perused with interest: –

"When I went among the Griquas, and for some time after, they were without the smallest marks of civilization. If I except one woman, (who had by some means got a bit of colonial raiment), they had not one thread of European clothing among them; and their wretched appearance and habits were such as must have excited in our minds an aversion to them had we not been actuated by principles which led us to pity them, and served to strengthen us in pursuing the object of our missionary work, – to restore beings sunk in many instances below the brutes. It is a fact, that we were among them at the hazard of our lives. This became evident to us by their own acknowledgments afterwards, they having confessed to us, that they had frequently premeditated to take away our lives, and that for that purpose they had taken weapons into their hands, and were prevented from executing their purposes by what they now considered an Almighty power.

"When we went among them, and for some time after, they lived in the habit of plundering each other, and they saw no moral evil in this, nor in any of their actions. Violent deaths were common; and I recollect many of the aged women told me their husbands had been killed in this way. Their usual manner of living was truly disgusting, and they were void of shame. However, after a series of hardships which required much faith and patience, our instructions were attended with a blessing which produced a great change. The people became honest in their dealings, they came to abhor those acts of plunder which had been so common among them; nor do I recollect a single instance for several years prior to their late troubles, which could be considered as a stain upon their character. They entirely abandoned their former manner of life, and decency and modesty prevailed in their families.

"One of the late chiefs of the Griquas told me one day, the following story. 'Sir,' said he, 'when you first came among us, I thought by myself – Come, I have no objections to have these Dutchmen among us; what they have will be ours; but if they think to persuade me to leave my wives and live as they do, that they shall discover shall never be able to effect. I will oppose it to the last. Little did I then think that my mind would ever be disposed to do such an act voluntarily; you never forced me to do this, it was my own act. Through hearing the word of God, I was convinced of sin, and induced to renounce it. Sir,' added he, 'you know little of the abominable lives we led, as we did all we could to keep you in the dark. When I look on my cattle, and think of my former life, I am ashamed.' The exemplary lives they then lived (adds Mr. Anderson) often made me ashamed of my own deficiencies.

"When we first settled among them we had some Hottentots with us from the Zak river. With their assistance we began to cultivate the ground about Riet Fonteyn; but notwithstanding our exhortations, remonstrations, and example, the Griquas manifested the greatest aversion to such work, and appeared determined to continue their wandering and predatory habits. At the end of six months the Hottentots left us, and our prospects as to the future cultivation of the ground became very gloomy. We determined, however, to abide by them; and in wandering about with them, we constantly endeavoured to impress upon their minds the superior advantages they would derive from cultivating the ground, and having fixed habitations. After a considerable time had elapsed, we prevailed upon them to try the experiment, and a commencement was made. This event was preceded and followed by a great and visible improvement upon them as a body. It was soon after our location in this place, that we were visited by Van der Graaf, Landdrost of Tulbagh, Mr. Van der Byl and Professor Lichtenstein. On this occasion, the Landdrost expressed himself thus: 'I find everything different from the reports which have reached the ears of the Governor; and I shall state to him the satisfaction I have felt, on finding things so different as they have been represented, on my return.'

"Considering the circumstances of the people, much land was cultivated at this time, and in the following years the land under cultivation was much increased. I have seen the whole valley from the Fountain down to Lion's Den (which must have included nearly four square miles) covered with corn and barley.

"This refers to Griqua Town alone, and the ground around the neighbouring fountains was in a similar state of improvement."

Before the Griquas were induced to give up their nomadic life and locate themselves in their present situation, the missionaries travelled about with them nearly five years, during which period such were their privations that they were often six months at a time without tasting bread. After they got the people to give up their wandering life, and they began to have bread and garden stuffs with their flesh, to use their own expression, "We seemed scarcely to have an earthly wish left that was not gratified." When, in addition to this improvement in their table, they got comfortable houses and clothing, and saw the people improving in their understandings, in piety and industry, they found their cup running over, and felt themselves repaid for all their sufferings and sacrifices.

Index

(Excluding the many references to William and Johanna Anderson, Griquatown and Pacaltsdorp)

Scripture References

William & Johanna Anderson — Genealogical Chart

Covering the period 1688 - 1852

Christofel Esterhuyzen (French Huguenot arrived Cape 1692) married Elisabeth Beijer (daughter of Andries Beijer and Catherine Vrijman of Stellenbosch)

Jan Andries Esterhuyzen married 27/7/1727 Appolonia Everts (daughter of French Huguenots Abraham Everts and Catherine Le Fevre)

Elizabeth Catharina Esterhuyzen

Jean du Plessis (French Huguenot arrived in Cape in 1688) married Marie Bruisset

Maria du Plessis married Johannes van Ellewee from Amsterdam

Hendrick Rudolf van Ellewee

married 7/12/1749

Elizabeth Maria van Ellewee (ⒷB 21/9/1750, ⒹD 10/6/1845)

married 10/11/1765

Johanna Maria Schonken (ⒷB Stellenbosch, 1776, ⒹD Pacaltsdorp 22/6/1848)

Bartholomeus Schonke(n) arrived in Cape in 1723; from Venlo, Holland, married Leonora Classen

Bartholomeus Schonken (ⒷB 1739)

William Anderson (ⒷB London 1/12/1769, ⒹD Pacaltsdorp 24/9/1852)

MARRIED 17 AUG 1806

William Anderson of Aberdeen

William Anderson (ⒷB 1724, merchant in London) married Catherine Turner of Devon 5/7/1768

1	2	3	4	5	6	7	8	9
William Bartholomew ⒷB Klaarwater 3/10/1807 ⒹD Cape Town 9/1/1810	Johannes Edward ⒷB Cape Town 24/7/1809	Maria Elizabeth ⒷB Cape Town 26/3/1811	Catherina Helen (Kitty) ⒷB Griquatown 9/9/1812	Johanna Wilhemena ⒷB Griquatown 30/12/1813	Elizabeth Anna ⒷB Griquatown 13/4/1816	Wilhemena Isabella ⒷB Griquatown 8/1/1818	Bartholomew Ebenezer ⒷB Griquatown 25/11/1819	George Peterus ⒷB George 11/3/1822 ⒹD Pacaltsdorp 1/6/1822
				married Daniel Helm, Jun 1835	married William Helm, Feb 1841		married Janet Melvill, 1842	

Ⓑ birth
Ⓓ died